PAINT IT TODAY

Editorial Board

The Cutting Edge:
Lesbian Life and Literature
General Editor: Karla Jay

H.D.
PAINT IT TODAY

Edited and with an Introduction
by Cassandra Laity

NEW YORK UNIVERSITY PRESS
New York and London

NEW YORK UNIVERSITY PRESS
New York and London

New York University Press gratefully acknowledges the
assistance of the Yale Collection of
American Literature, Benecke Rare
Book and Manuscript Library,
Yale University.

Library of Congress Cataloging-in-Publication Data
H. D. (Hilda Doolittle), 1886–1961.
Paint it today / H.D. ; edited and with an introduction by
Cassandra Laity.
p.   cm.—The Cutting edge)
Includes bibliographical references and index.
ISBN 0-8147-3487-1 alk. paper)--ISBN 0-8147-3488-X
(pbk. : alk. paper)
I. Laity, Cassandra.   II. Title.   III. Series: Cutting edge (New York, N.Y.)
PS3507.0726P28   1992   92-6150
813'.52—dc20   CIP

New York University Press books are printed on acid-free paper,
and their binding materials are chosen for strength and durability.

Manufactured in the United States of America

c 10 9 8 7 6 5 4 3 2 1
p 10 9 8 7 6 5 4 3 2 1

Contents

Foreword

Karla Jay

Professor of English and Women's Studies
Pace University

Despite the efforts of lesbian and feminist publishing houses and a few university presses, the bulk of the most important lesbian works has traditionally been available only from rare book dealers, in a few university libraries, or in gay and lesbian archives. This series intends, in the first place, to make representative examples of this neglected and insufficiently known literature available to a broader audience by reissuing selected classics and by putting into print for the first time lesbian novels, diaries, letters, and memoirs that have special interest and significance, but which have moldered in libraries and private collections for decades or even for centuries, known only to the few scholars who had the courage and financial wherewithal to track them down.

Their names have been known for a long time—Sappho, the

Amazons of North Africa, the Beguines, Aphra Behn, Queen Christina, Emily Dickinson, the Ladies of Llangollen, Radclyffe Hall, Natalie Clifford Barney, H.D. . . . and so many others from every nation, race, and era. But government and religious officials burned their writings, historians and literary scholars denied they were lesbians, powerful men kept their books out of print, and influential archivists locked up their ideas far from sympathetic eyes. Yet, some dedicated scholars and readers still knew who they were, made pilgrimages to the cities and villages where they had lived and to the graveyards where they rested. They passed around tattered volumes of letters, diaries, and biographies, in which they had underlined what seemed to be telltale hints of a secret or different kind of life. Where no hard facts existed, legends were invented. The few precious and often available pre-Stonewall lesbian classics, such as *The Well of Loneliness* by Radclyffe Hall, *The Price of Salt* by Claire Morgan [Patricia Highsmith], and *Desert of the Heart* by Jane Rule, were cherished. Lesbian pulp was devoured. One of the primary goals of this series is to give the more neglected works, which actually constitute the vast majority of lesbian writing, the attention they deserve.

A second but no less important aim of this series is to present the "cutting edge" of contemporary lesbian scholarship and theory across a wide range of disciplines. Practitioners of lesbian studies have not adopted a uniform approach to literary theory, history, sociology, or any other discipline, nor should they. This series intends to present an array of voices that truly reflect the diversity of the lesbian community. To help me in this task, I am lucky enough to be assisted by a distinguished editorial board that reflects various professional, class, racial, ethnic, and religious backgrounds as well as a spectrum of interests and sexual preferences.

At present lesbian studies occupies a small, precarious, and somewhat contested pied-à-terre between gay studies and women's studies. The former is still in its infancy, especially if one compares it to other disciplines that have been part of the core curriculum of every child and adolescent for several decades or even centuries. However, while one of the newest, gay studies may also be the fastest-growing discipline—at least in North America. Lesbian, gay, and bisexual studies conferences are doubling or tripling their attendance. While only a handful of degree-granting programs currently exist, that number is also apt to multiply quickly in the next decade.

In comparison, women's studies is a well-established and burgeoning discipline with hundreds of minors, majors, and graduate programs throughout the United States. Lesbian studies occupies a peripheral place in the curricula of such programs, characteristically restricted to one lesbian-centered course, usually literary or historical in nature. In the many women's studies series that are now offered by university presses, generally only one or two books on a lesbian subject or issue are included in each series, and lesbian voices are restricted to writing on those topics considered of special interest to gay people. We are not called upon to offer our opinions on motherhood, war, education or on the lives of women not publicly identified as lesbians. As a result, lesbian experience is too often marginalized and restricted.

In contrast, this series will prioritize, centralize, and celebrate lesbian visions of literature, art, philosophy, love, religion, ethics, history, and a myriad of other topics. In "The Cutting Edge," readers can find authoritative versions of important lesbian texts that have been carefully prepared and introduced by scholars. Readers can also find the work of academics and independent scholars who write passionately about lesbian studies and issues or who write about other aspects of life from a distinctly lesbian viewpoint. These visions are not only various but intentionally contradictory, for lesbians speak from differing class, racial, ethnic, and religious perspectives. Each author also speaks from and about a certain moment of time, and few would argue that being a lesbian today is the same as it was for Sappho or Anne Lister. Thus, no attempt has been made to homogenize that diversity, and no agenda exists to attempt to carve out a "politically correct" lesbian studies perspective at this juncture in history or to pinpoint the "real" lesbians in history. It seems more important for all the voices to be heard before those with the blessings of aftersight lay the mantle of authenticity on any one vision of the world, or on any particular set of women.

What each work in this series does share, however, is a common realization that gay women are the "Other" and that one's perception of culture and literature is filtered by sexual behaviors and preferences. Those perceptions are not the same as those of gay men or of nongay women, whether the writers speak of gay or feminist issues or whether the writers choose to look at nongay figures from a lesbian perspective. The role of this series is to create space and give a voice to those interested in lesbian studies. This series speaks to any person who is interested in gender studies, literary criticism, biography, or important literary works, whether she or he is a student, professor, or serious reader, for it is not for lesbians only or even by lesbians only. Instead, "The Cutting Edge" attempts to share some of the best of lesbian literature and lesbian studies with anyone willing to look at the world through our eyes. The series is proactive in that it will help to formulate and foreground the very discipline on which it focuses. Finally, this series has answered the call to make lesbian theory, lesbian experience, lesbian lives, lesbian literature, and lesbian visions the heart and nucleus, the weighty planet around which for once other viewpoints will swirl as moons to our earth. We invite readers of all persuasions to join us by venturing into this and other books in the series.

Like so many other works containing homoerotic themes— such as E. M. Forster's *Maurice* and Gertrude Stein's *Q.E.D.*— *Paint It Today* here receives its first publication, all too long after the death of H.D. (Hilda Doolittle). Though H.D.'s lesbian affairs have received far less attention than her relationships with Ezra Pound and Richard Aldington, her lesboerotic passions take center stage in this lyrical novella, as H.D. explores her love for Frances Gregg and Bryher, two women in whom she sought both love and family as well as an emotional partnership. This autobiographical memoir adds new dimension to an increasingly appreciated author and will enthrall those who are discovering H.D. here for the first time. It will delight her already dedicated fans as well.

Acknowledgments

I wish to thank Susan Stanford Friedman for her indispensable corrections and suggestions on the near-final draft of the Introduction. I am also grateful to Eileen Gregory and James Hala, whose ready knowledge of everything helped me track down some of H.D.'s more obscure references.

CASSANDRA LAITY

Lesbian Romanticism: H.D.'s Fictional Representations of Frances Gregg and Bryher

Cassandra Laity

Paint It Today, a roman à clef by the American poet H.D. (Hilda Doolittle), is one of three autobiographical novels (including *Asphodel* and *HER*) exploring H.D.'s love for women. With this edition the publication of H.D.'s most overtly homoerotic novels is complete.[1] None of the novels was published in H.D.'s lifetime (she labeled the typescript of *Asphodel* "DESTROY"), the manuscript of *Paint It Today* appears to be unfinished, and at this writing the publication of both *Asphodel* and *Paint It Today* is still in progress. The H.D. that emerges from these "private" writings reveals a story she suppressed in her poetry—a largely biographical account in which one woman, Frances Gregg, figures as the most compelling erotic and emotional love-experience of H.D.'s life, and another woman, Bryher, as her protectorate, "child," and life partner. *Paint It Today* is a mythic, lyrical re-creation of H.D.'s love and loss of Gregg, her first woman lover, and her later meeting with Bryher (Winifred Ellerman). Spanning the years from H.D.'s childhood in Pennsylvania to the birth of her daughter Perdita in 1919, the homoerotic love story of *Paint It Today* is set against the backdrop of World War I, H.D.'s involvement with the literary circles in London, her brief engagement to American poet Ezra Pound, and her shattered marriage to British novelist Richard Aldington. However, readers have described *Paint It Today* as H.D.'s most "lesbian" novel: a modern homoerotic novel of passage, *Paint It Today* focuses entirely on the young heroine's search for the "sister love" who would empower her spiritually, sexually, and creatively. The "stories" of H.D.'s brief engagement to Pound ("Raymond") and her marriage to Aldington ("Basil") are relegated to the background, while the narrative dwells exclusively on H.D.'s very differently defined love for the sexually magnetic, betraying Gregg and for the more nurturing and loyal Bryher.

This H.D., who imaginatively and actually chose a lesbian existence and who confronted the psychological and social dynamics of a lesbian identity in her writing, has been largely unavailable to many of her readers. As H.D.'s letters[2] and fiction appear in print through the efforts of series such as The Cutting Edge, we are able to consider the nature of H.D.'s lesbian identity and of her relationships with Bryher and Gregg in the context of early modern lesbian literature. However, H.D. remains somewhat difficult to "place."

Divergent "Selves"

Even a brief outline of H.D.'s turbulent biography reveals a diversity of "selves." Born in America, H.D. spent most of her life in England. Best known for her spare, "Imagist" poetry and her romantic associations with Ezra Pound, Richard Aldington,

D. H. Lawrence and other originators of "male" literary modernism, H.D. also lived with Bryher off and on for twenty-seven
years (1919–1946), was a lesbian mother, and wrote homoerotic,
feminist fiction and poetry.

Hilda Doolittle was born in Pennsylvania in 1886, the daughter of an astronomy professor, Charles Doolittle, and a former
art and music teacher, Helen Wolle Doolittle.[3] At fifteen she
met Ezra Pound, to whom she was engaged intermittently through
her early twenties. During this time H.D. attended Bryn Mawr
College but subsequently withdrew (discouraged by her failing
grades) in her sophomore year (1906). Four years later, confused
by the failure of her college career, her sometime engagements
to Ezra Pound, and the growing disapproval of her parents,
H.D. met and fell in love with Frances Gregg (1910), the "muse"
who alerted the young H.D. to her poetic vocation and the
woman whom H.D. would consistently describe as the love of
her life. H.D., Gregg, and Gregg's mother traveled to Europe
in 1911, where H.D. became involved in the active London
literary circles and helped start the Imagist poetic movement
that included Pound, Richard Aldington, and others. A year after
their arrival in London, H.D. was surprised and stunned by
Gregg's sudden unexplained desertion and marriage to lecturer
Louis Wilkinson. Shortly thereafter, H.D. married Richard Aldington (1913). During the next few eventful years, World War I
broke out and H.D. suffered the stillbirth of their child (1915).
Her first volume of Imagist poems, *Sea Garden*, was published
in 1916, and H.D. was immediately recognized as the most
"perfect" exemplar of Imagism—a credo based on the (presumably) genderless, precise rendering of a visual image. Throughout their six-year cohabitation,[4] Aldington engaged in several
adulterous affairs, and his open relationship with Dorothy Yorke
dissolved the marriage. They separated, after which H.D. briefly
lived with musician Cecil Gray in Cornwall; when she became
pregnant, she moved out. She met Bryher during this period
(1918): the women mutually believed that their ordained meet-

ing had saved both their lives—Bryher from suicide because of her parents' overprotectiveness, and H.D. from the life-threatening influenza that nearly killed her and her unborn child in 1919. Both mother and child were saved by Bryher's intervention. Frances Perdita (named after Gregg) was born in March, and Bryher adopted the child. Their union inspired H.D.'s second volume of poetry, *Hymen* (1921) (dedicated to Bryher and Perdita), as well as H.D.'s fictional celebrations of lesbian love, *Paint It Today* (composed in 1921), *Asphodel* (1921–1922), and *HER* (1926–1927). Until 1946 H.D. would divide her time between her "family" and various residences in Europe. During the 1930s H.D. published poetry, wrote novels, stories, essays, and copious letters; participated in the avante-garde cinema; and became Freud's analysand in 1933. In the 1940s, H.D. and Bryher lived through the Blitz of World War II in London, which she mythologized in her epic poem, *Trilogy* (1942–1944). In the next decade H.D. wrote her second major long poem, *Helen in Egypt* (1952–1955). Although H.D. never married again and she and Bryher remained companions until H.D.'s death at age seventy-five in 1961, they never presented themselves publicly as anything more than "cousins." H.D. continued to pursue serious flirtations and affairs with men, and Bryher married twice, largely to mask her sexual orientation.

H.D.'s place in the lesbian literary milieu of the early twentieth century has been obscured largely, therefore, because of the unavailability of her prose, her several public relationships with famous men, her association with (male) high modernism, and H.D.'s guarded attitude about her relationship with Bryher.[5] H.D. was always secretive about her lesbianism: as a friend of H.D.'s recently disclosed, H.D. and her lesbian friends were deeply disturbed by the outrage over Radclyffe Hall's court case and did not dare to "call" themselves "homosexuals." ("We had to be very, very careful," H.D.'s friend recalls.)[6] During her marriage H.D. admitted to a fashionable bisexuality, a penchant for what Aldington described as "girl loves" that was considered titillating in the Bohemian atmosphere of the London literary circles.

However, potential readers and publishers (then and now) may also have been put off because H.D.'s extremely coded, mythic, and lyrical quest-novels for the "sister love" do not, initially, fit any immediately recognizable forms of early modern homoerotic fiction. *Paint It Today* is too exclusively "lesbian" (it valorizes the love of women over men) to be considered among the World War I novels dwelling on the bisexual *liaisons* of the London literary circle—many of which were written by H.D.'s friends.[7] On the other hand, H.D.'s "sister love" eludes the more male-identified conceptions of lesbianism characteristic of such early modern classics as Radclyffe Hall's *Well of Loneliness.* As critics have pointed out, although *Paint It Today, HER,* and *Asphodel* were written during the 1920s, unlike Hall's Stephen, H.D.'s "sister love" does not demonstrate the influence of sexologist Havelock Ellis's then-popular definition of lesbianism as a "congenital inversion" that "traps a man in a woman's body."[8] For several reasons, therefore, H.D.'s lesbian identity has not been highly "visible." In order to understand the personal, social, and psychological dynamics of the lesbian identity that H.D. re-created in novels such as *Paint It Today,* it is important to recognize the system of "codes" she uses to differentiate and articulate modes and levels of lesbian desire. In the remainder of this Introduction I would like to discuss how the lesbian Romanticism of H.D.'s homoerotic fiction, particularly in *Paint It Today,* debates conflicting forms of lesbian love and existence (represented by Bryher and Gregg) through Romantic myths and "codes" for transgressive desire.

The "Sister"/"Mother" Love: Romantic Encodings

Early in both *Paint It Today* and *HER,* H.D. establishes her young heroines' lesbian desire as a half-conceived longing for "a twin self sister," "the half of herself that was forever missing"

(*HER* 10, 16): "She wanted most passionately a girl child of her own age, a twin sister. . . . This particular yearning for one child, a girl of its own particular temperament, was satisfied when Midget had left school, had left childhood, girlhood; was drifting unsatisfied, hurt and baffled out of a relationship with a hectic, adolescent, blundering . . . youth" (*Paint It Today* 7). Later in *Paint It Today*, Midget's wistful letter to the departed Josepha (based on Frances Gregg) calls up the maternal eroticism of their relationship through references to an eroticized, mythical "mother," Artemis: "[Artemis's] face was like our mother's face. She was sister to our mother. She culled us close to her, more loving than a mother, because her arms were hungry. Nothing would ease her heart. Almost we loved her more than our lost mother because her heart was always unappeased. Almost we would give her anything to make her smile" (57).

While H.D.'s "sister"/"mother" love does not fit Ellis's model, her homoerotic fictions of the self-identifying female *eros* affiliate her with those "texts" described by Catharine Stimpson's overview of the lesbian novel, in which "characters" "search . . . for alter egos, moral and psychological equivalents which the term "sister" [and/or "mother"] signifies" (Stimpson 256).[9] In the context of an early modern "tradition," H.D.'s use of Romantic myths of androgyny and "the great mother" to encode transgressive desire allies her with the lesbian Romanticism of writers such as Renée Vivien, Colette, and Natalie Barney. These writers drew upon the Romantic philosophy of love as a union between "twin" androgynous spirits (initially male and female) in their articulations of the self-identifying "sister" or "mother" love. Influenced particularly by Decadent aesthetes such as Charles Baudelaire and A. C. Swinburne, Vivien, Barney, and others looked back to their sexually transgressive "mothers," classical figures such as Sappho, or the Greek goddess Artemis, and to the sisterhoods/matriarchies of Lesbos, the Amazons, and others.[10] Furthermore, writers such as H.D. and Renée Vivien were strongly attracted to the converse Romantic image of the "terrible mother," the often lesbian femme fatale who projected a powerful female sexuality in works such as Baudelaire's *Les Fleurs du Mal* or Swinburne's poem "Anactoria" in *Poems and Ballads*. H.D., Vivien, and others appear to have adapted these differently conceived images of the Romantic "twin," represented, for example, by Artemis (goddess of the Amazons) and the Decadent femme fatale, in order to debate important personal, creative, and psychological issues of their lesbian existence.

Indeed, H.D.'s and Renée Vivien's romans à clef of their devastating relationships with, respectively, Frances Gregg and Natalie Barney cast their first loves as all-consuming femmes fatales while the more nurturing, sympathetic lovers that succeeded them are contrastingly depicted as the vigorous members of self-sustaining, pastoral, communities of women. In Vivien's *A Woman Appeared to Me*, Barney is a Decadent fatal woman dressed in seductive silks and transparent gauze. Her eyes "blue and piercing as a blade," she "radiat[es] the charm of danger" (*A Woman* 2). Vally's (Barney's) announcement of her engagement to a man drives the distracted narrator to nervous collapse. She is, however, rescued by the timely appearance of a woman appropriately named "Eva" (a composite of several women in Vivien's life) who inspires Edenic fantasies of "fresh green silence, . . . living water and forests . . . beyond the ugliness of the city" (*A Woman* 33). This contrast between the often violent sexuality of the femme fatale and the more sensuous eros of the utopic Sapphic community is also present in Vivien's poetry, which mingles poems to a sadistic Parisian "maîtresse" with poems celebrating a Mytilene (Lesbos) of gentle lovers and "azure" skies.[11]

H.D.'s *Paint It Today* inscribes a similar opposition in the figures represented by Gregg and Bryher. *Paint It Today* begins by mythologizing Gregg as the primary sister/mother love who awoke the young H.D. to her poetic and sexual powers in their native Pennsylvania. However, benevolent Romantic images of

Artemisian androgyny and mother/sister love give way progressively to female icons of "vice" after Josepha (Gregg) suddenly abandons Midget (H.D.) in a surprise marriage to a British lecturer (based on Louis Wilkinson, whom Gregg married in 1912). Although H.D.'s Josepha conjures fatal women throughout the novel, the emotionally devastated heroine begins to perceive Josepha exclusively as Hecate, queen of hell (the "dark" aspect of Artemis), a witch, and the lesbian femme fatale "Faustine" of Swinburne's poem (to be discussed later). Like Vivien's Edenic Eva, the woman who "appears" in *A Woman Appeared to Me*, Midget's lesbian redeemer, white Althea (based on Bryher), suddenly materializes in a Sapphic utopia at the end of *Paint It Today*. There Midget, exhausted by war and the loss of Josepha, rediscovers love, community, and freedom. In an uncharacteristically bold encoding of lesbian sexuality, H.D. depicts the two women as naked "daughters of Artemis," joyfully battling a storm-wracked landscape: "The feel of it. The bite and tear and sting of it. . . . All the power of the wood seemed to circle between those two alert and vivid bodies" (84).

Feminist readers have attributed Vivien's fascination with the femme fatale in particular to her internalization of the "doomed lesbian" image.[12] However, I believe that H.D. and Vivien also used the initially "male" dichotomy to debate different forms of lesbian love. Gregg and Bryher occupy radically diverse positions in H.D.'s fiction. While both are reminiscent of the lost mother/sister her heroines seek, they are also antithetical "muses," each representing divergent forms of sexuality and lesbian existence, and each crucial to the development of the poet-heroine at differing stages of her life.[13] Thus H.D.'s youthful heroine's all-consuming attachment to the poetic, sexually magnetic, and telepathic femme fatale (Gregg) in *HER* and *Paint It Today* forms the powerful, catalyzing force behind her decision to oppose "female" convention and seek her vocation as a poet. Later, after H.D.'s world-weary heroines have survived the ravages of war, the loss of Gregg, and the dissolution of marriage, the Artemisian Bryher-figure offers, among other things, the much-needed community of kindred spirits that enables H.D.'s poet heroines to write again. (H.D., Bryher, and H.D.'s daughter Perdita had formed a nonconventional family shortly before *Paint It Today* was composed.)

Moreover, the Romantic lesbian femme fatale also provided H.D. and Vivien with an effective image for the painful consequences attendant upon a female intimacy modeled too closely after the mother-daughter dyad. H.D.'s critics have uncovered the problematics of H.D.'s relationships with men; most notably, Rachel Blau DuPlessis's article, "Romantic Thralldom in H.D.," demonstrates the passively "feminine," "all-encompassing, totally defining love" that characterized H.D.'s attachments to her male mentors and threatened to efface her as a poet (406). However, I would like to examine a pattern of "thralldom" more particular to female same-sex love—which H.D. experienced in her relationship with Frances Gregg, and from which Bryher provided an enabling escape.

Both H.D. and Vivien[14] fixed on the image of the fatal woman because they mutually perceived the intensity of Gregg's and Barney's love as a form of erotic thralldom. I suggest that their inscriptions of the fatal woman articulate a specific phenomenon of some lesbian relationships that too closely replicate the mother-daughter bond. Psychotherapist Joyce P. Lindenbaum observes that in these couples, one woman may feel that she has become "lost in her partner": "Along with the blissful experience of mother-infant oneness comes the terror of possible identity loss, object-loss and complete dependence" (Lindenbaum 86). Lindenbaum cites Nancy Chodorow's theory that this form of symbiosis is more apt to emerge in woman-to-woman intimacies because they most closely replicate the mother-daughter bond. "How can," Lindenbaum continues, "the women fulfill their original desire to merge, and simultaneously subdue the terror it arises?" (86). H.D.'s *Paint It Today* addresses this particular question in its debate between an all-consuming mother-love

(Gregg) and a more nurturing, communal, and less engulfing sister/mother bond (Bryher). I suggest that women writers such as Vivien and H.D., therefore, "used" the powerful image of the femme fatale to embody their "terror" of a simultaneously appropriating and rejecting "mother." Catharine Stimpson notes that the wrenching breakup of "the mother-daughter exchange" that once inspired a return to "primal origins . . . primal loves" is a familiar topic of lesbian literature. H.D.'s and Vivien's choice of the "horrific" femme fatale to image their faithless first loves seems appropriate to Stimpson's macabre description of the psychic violence of these texts wherein the lover's jealousy "spurts like blood from the cut of terror" (Stimpson 256, 257).

Frances Gregg

Frances Josepha Gregg was born in 1884 and was two years older than H.D. She lived with her widowed mother, a schoolteacher, in Philadelphia. H.D. and Gregg were introduced by a mutual friend from Bryn Mawr four years after H.D.'s withdrawal. The passionate relationship that ensued is the focus of H.D.'s *HER* and *Paint It Today*. Both novels associate Gregg with the same wrenching narrative of first love and creative flowering followed by betrayal and madness/despair despite the different time periods they cover: *HER* dwells on the early years of the young women's first meeting in Pennsylvania and the dramatic impact on H.D. of Gregg's unexpected proclamation of love for H.D.'s then-fiancé Ezra Pound; and *Paint It Today* follows the couple to Europe with Gregg's mother after H.D.'s broken engagement, where Gregg "betrayed" H.D. for the last time by leaving London to marry lecturer Louis Wilkinson.

There is no sharp division between the classical/Romantic imagery of Artemisian goddesses or beautiful youths and the sinister femmes fatales that cumulatively signal the controlling power of H.D.'s Frances Gregg in *HER* and *Paint It Today*. Gregg's ability to draw out the young H.D.'s mythopoeic powers arose as much from Gregg's brooding, "dark" sensuality, her fascination with prophecy, witchcraft, and other supernatural forces (in the novels they call themselves "wee witches") as from their mutually sustaining sisterhood. H.D. perceived her deep enthrallment with the young Frances Gregg as partly responsible for her enduring vocation as a poet. While the fiancé (Pound) in *Paint It Today* and *HER* gropes clumsily at his fiancée and ridicules her emerging gift—"Your pomes *[sic]* are rotten" (167) —the Gregg-figures create a mystic atmosphere for Hermione's newly discovered powers. Poetry readings, "visions," and caresses characterize Hermione's and Fayne's "sessions" in Hermione's workroom, transporting her into "other" worlds of poetic, visionary, and sensual experience. These ritual "sessions," which generated an aesthetic of "sister love" from Romantic poetry and classical images of androgyny, would remain a compelling site of poetic inspiration throughout H.D.'s career. Before discussing the femme fatale, I will begin with a brief examination of the more "benign" Romantic imagery attending H.D.'s fictional renderings of Gregg.

In H.D.'s fiction where homoerotic passion often appears to underlie all poetic expression, coded references to the "sister love" she shared with Gregg become synonymous with poetry itself. H.D. and Gregg read Swinburne's "Itylus," which emphasizes the sister-bond between the Procne and Philomel of Greek myth, almost obsessively to each other during their early intimacy, until the poem and particularly its refrain—"sister, my sister, O fleet, sweet swallow"—became their ode to lesbian love (Swinburne 187–189). (Philomel served her son Itylus to her husband, Tereus, for dinner in order to revenge Tereus's rape and mutilation of her sister, whereupon the gods changed the sisters into the nightingale and the swallow.) Midget divines a lesbian muse behind the most affecting poetry, which she repeatedly links with references to the (sister) "swallow." During a rapt meditation on lyric poetry, Midget professes her dislike for the implicitly "masculine," "epic" style, while she prefers those (presumably "feminine") "songs that cut like a *swallow* wing the high, untainted ether . . . [imitating] the beat and drop of poetry, the swerve up and the *swallow* wing beating back" (11, 10; italics mine). Later, baffled by war and the double loss of Josepha and her husband, Midget attempts to revive the poetic spirit of the "sister" love by recalling Swinburne's poem to her estranged friend. She writes imploringly to the now-married and pregnant Josepha, "Have people forgotten what poetry is? You used to know what poetry is? Do you remember how you made me say 'Swallow' . . . to you? Do you remember 'the wild birds, take flight and follow and find the sun'?" (55–56). In *HER,* Philomel's plaintive call to her sister swallow haunts both the erotic and creative union of the lovers; lying across the body of the sleeping Fayne, Hermione imagines their hearts beating to the rhythm of the poem: "*O sister my sister O fleet sweet swallow* ran rhythm of her head . . . beat rhythm of a heart that beat and beat" (180; H.D.'s emphasis). Indeed, Swinburne's refrain, "sister, my sister, O fleet sweet swallow," echoes erratically throughout H.D.'s poetry and prose, invoking the call to the lost lesbian muse even in "heterosexual" works such as the late poem, *Helen in Egypt.*[15]

H.D. and Gregg also perceived icons of the "sister love" in the androgynous Grecian "boys" the Decadents had derived from Greek nude statuary in their own coded poems to male transgressive desire.[16] Frances Gregg covered H.D.'s copy of her first volume, *Sea Garden,* with handwritten poems to H.D., including an ode to H.D.'s androgynous beauty, which she entitled after Swinburne's lyric portrait of a "boy" hermaphrodite, "Hermaphroditus" (Swinburne 213). H.D. herself treasured the small, childlike statue of the *Hermaphrodite,* which had inspired Swinburne; and she later enshrined a representation of the sculpture she had seen in the Diocletian gallery in her home beside a picture of Bryher. In *Paint It Today,* the now-married Midget sees the prewar image of a former homoerotic "self" in "the gentle breathing" figure of the *Hermaphrodite,* "modeled in strange, soft, honey-colored stone" (65). Furthermore, the sensuous passion for Greek statuary itself that became a code for (male) homoeroticism in Wilde and Pater (Pater mentions the historian Winckelmann fingering "those pagan marbles [of male nudes]" "with no sense of shame or loss"), becomes a code for female-female love in *Paint It Today*.[17]

Chapter Six, entitled "Sister of Charmides," refers obliquely to Oscar Wilde's poem "Charmides," in which the legend of a fair youth's obsessive love for a goddess's statue is used to signify homoeroticism. H.D.'s designation of Midget as a "sister" of Charmides manipulates the Decadent code to articulate female desire. Midget imaginatively becomes a "sister" of Charmides (or of Pater's Winckelmann) during her visit to the "incandescent," larger-than-life statue of the *Venus de Milo:* she apprehends the sculpture with eyes that long to trace, like fingers, "the curve of the white belly and short space before the breasts brought the curve to a sudden shadow"; but she "dared not" betray "the whitest passion" while in the company of the uncomprehending Basil (i.e., Aldington) (60).

Finally, as Susan Friedman demonstrates in *Penelope's Web*, Artemis is the presiding genius of the "sister/mother" mythos H.D. created first with Gregg and later with Bryher. The goddess dominates the narrative of *Paint It Today*, figuring "female independence and rebellion against the desire of men" as well as homoerotic love (*PW* 191). As Midget's "Artemis," Josepha is both the wild, fleet-footed "twin sister" whom H.D.'s heroines yearn for and the object of Midget's insatiable longing for a maternal beloved, the "sister to our mother" that Midget mourns in the above-mentioned wistful letter to Josepha.

H.D.'s "Thralldom" to Frances Gregg: The Femme Fatale. However, as Midget bitterly reminds Josepha, Artemis "was Hecate in hell" (56). The exclusivity of the mother/sister bond that enabled H.D.'s heroines to explore the mythopoeic mind also paradoxically holds them in thrall. In H.D.'s re-creations of her "romantic thralldom" to men, her heroines feel "obliterated" (H.D.'s word) by the gender barriers that divide the sexes; but H.D.'s lesbian heroine and her "twin self sister" struggle for autonomy from within a stifling "sameness." The new creative/ erotic "self" Hermione acquires through Fayne is both empowering and annihilating, inspiring both "the blissful experience of mother-infant oneness" and "the terror" of "identity loss and complete dependence" that Lindenbaum describes. At times the amoeboid boundaries between Hermione and her mother/sister muse are so fluid that the "self" appears bewilderingly evasive: after a confrontation with Fayne (and Fayne's mother) Hermione grasps for her new identity, repeating confusedly to herself, "I know her. Her [Hermione]. I am Her. She is Her. Knowing her I know Her. She is some amplification of myself like amoeba giving birth, by breaking off, to amoeba. I am a sort of mother, a sort of sister to her." At worst, however, Hermione feels lost to a demonic, consuming "mother."

The Femme Fatale. From the moment she appears in *Paint It Today,* Josepha is suggestive of the deceiving femme fatale. Midget's first impression of Josepha notes the disconcerting "unwholesome" pallor, and texture of her face, which belies the heavenly promise of her eyes:

The other girl's face was slightly spotted. Her color was bad. . . . It was her eyes [that captivated Midget], set in the unwholesome face . . . it was her eyes, an unholy spendor.
    Her eyes were the blue eyes it is said one sees in heaven; eyes, Angelo would have garnered in a group of holy boys. . . . eyes [of] . . . bright steel; eyes the color of wet hyacinths before the spikes have broken into flower. (9)

Elsewhere Pound would comment that Gregg's face reminded of a Burne Jones fury; and indeed the ominous juxtaposition of dazzling, hypnotic eyes against deathly pallor is reminiscent of the pre-Raphaelite femme fatale. (Vivien's Barney in *A Woman*

Appeared to Me is also notably pale, with "ice blue eyes.")
H.D.'s harsher depictions of Gregg would cite her "water blue
eyes and stricken features" as evidence of Gregg's cruelty and
neurosis (*Narthex* 231). However, initially the slightly sinister
cast of the Gregg-figure's face suggests only what Vivien describes in *A Woman Appeared to Me* as "the charm of danger"
(2).

In both H.D.'s and Vivien's fictional reminiscences of Gregg
and Barney, the femme fatale's increasing dominion threatens
metaphorically to consume or "drown" them. During the "kiss"
scene [18] that encodes the lesbian sexuality of *HER*, Hermione's
"session" with Fayne takes on the aspect of a satanic rite. As the
women approach each other, Hermione is drawn inexorably by
the hypnotic eyes and face of a demonic femme fatale. Hermione's workroom imaginatively transforms into a decadent bou-
doir and Fayne appears to assume the "mask" of Swinburne's
scarred lesbian femme fatale Faustine, a debauched Roman empress. The poem's refrain, "lips long since half kissed away,"
which refers to the empress's worn imprint on a gold coin, both
encodes the kiss and suggests the "decadent" atmosphere that
holds Hermione captive:

I feel the fringe of some fantastic wine-colored parting curtains. Curtains part as I look into the eyes of Fayne Rabb . . . curtains parted,
curtains filled the air with heavy swooping purple. Lips long since half
kissed away. Curled lips long since half kissed away. . . . Long ere they
coined in Roman gold your face—your face—your face—your face—
your face—Faustine. (165)

Overwhelmed by the kiss, Hermione feels as if they "had fallen
into a deep well and were looking up." In *A Woman Appeared
to Me* Vivien describes Vally's sensuous impact on the narrator
similarly as "the luminous dizziness which comes at the edge of
an abyss, or the attraction of a very deep water" (2).

The metaphors of confinement that accompany H.D.'s depic-
tion of her enchantment with Gregg certainly reflect the young

H.D.'s fears about the "hidden" "perversity" of her first lesbian experience. However, they also suggest the exclusivity and isolation of their sister/mother bond. The women's rejection of the outside world clearly contributes to Midget's impression that they are "cast out of the mass of the living," "separated" even from the Bohemian and presumably lesbian communities of artists in London (*Paint It Today* 18). As Karla Jay notes, Renée Vivien's decadent femme fatale, Aphrodite, is an "indoor goddess" whose "temple is dark and cloistral" (Jay 77). Indeed, Vivien's claustrophobic description in the poem "Venus" of Aphrodite's dramatic entrance recalls the staging of Fayne's kiss in Hermione's workroom, "The foliage parts like the folds of curtains/ Before the Venus of the Blind" (Jay 77). Thus, in contrast to the expansive, storm-wracked landscape that encodes the more liberating sensuality of the H.D.-Bryher pairing in *Paint It Today*, the H.D.-Gregg couplings of *Paint It Today* and *HER* remain indoors. Her and Fayne meet only in the small, tense space of Hermione's workroom, although Farrand forest lies just outside. Significantly, Midget declares to Althea that she and Josepha have never seen each other naked "out of doors" —their attempt to "watch" one another in an old boat is foiled when a "man" appears. And in *Paint It Today* we see the lovers in the dark, antique atmosphere of museums where Midget and Josepha's mother, Julia, are locked in a tight contest for Josepha's attention.

Finally, Catharine Stimpson's evocative description of the psychic wounding—"like blood from the cut of terror"—that takes place in the lesbian texts that treat the breakup of the "mother/daughter exchange" is appropriate to H.D.'s most embittered re-creations of Gregg as the betraying femme fatale. Gregg's sexual betrayal(s) and thus her abuse of the mother/daughter bond she formed with H.D. seemed to cut closer to the bone even than Aldington's desertion. While men distanced and trivialized H.D.-the-poet, by idealizing her as the passive "muse," Gregg "ripped souls from bodies," intimately nourish-

ing H.D.'s creative spirit only to "blight" it later. In *Narthex*,
written shortly after *HER* in 1927 or 1928, Gregg is likened to a
sadistic "Venus" who nurtures and then violates the psychic
"Adonis" gardens of her victims: "Katherine brought tiny roots
out, Adonis garden to be swiftly withered. One was all Adon-
garden under Katherine's regime, all sudden premature spiritual
flowering, to be as prematurely blighted. Katherine ripped souls
from bodies . . . would condemn you to an eternity of abandon-
ment, emotional starvation" (231). Similarly, in a 1930 letter to
Bryher, H.D. described Gregg as "a psychic klepto-maniac. She
must get and break" ("Two Loves" 228). While the Aldington-
figures of H.D.'s fiction leave her heroines in a benumbed state
of self-effacement (in "Murex," *Bid Me to Live*, and other works),
Fayne's betrayal in *HER* ravages Hermione body and soul, sending her into long-term illness and raving dementia. At the conclusion of the manuscript of *Paint It Today*, Midget bitterly
pronounces her sometime "sisterhood" with Josepha as noxious
and obscuring, "ghostly as the sulphurous substance they call in
London winter, fog" (89).

Still, even Gregg's "terrible" aspect continued to fuel H.D.'s
imagination long after the relationship had ended. At nearly fifty
years of age, H.D. wrote to a friend that she was "still liv[ing]
down" her love for "Frances," a love she described as "terrible
with banners . . . [that] only emerges or materializes once or
twice in a lifetime" (Guest 228).

Bryher

The concluding celebratory phase of H.D.'s romance-plots often
introduces a type of Bryher presiding over a "Greek" island-
paradise of revitalizing light, air, and water. This pastoral scene
of "rescue" appears repeatedly in H.D.'s autobiographical fiction
and serves as an antedote to both heterosexual "romantic thralldom" and to what I have been describing as H.D.'s homoerotic
thralldom to Gregg. Appended to the heterosexual narrative of

Asphodel or the stories in *Palimpsest,* the female paradise valorizes lesbian love and the self-identifying eros over the conven-
tionally divisive, unequal relation between the sexes. However,
as an alternative to Gregg, in the homoerotic narratives of *Paint
It Today* or *Asphodel,* the Bryher-figure and her woman-centered coastal "communities" offer release from the isolating exclusivity and terror of loss that accompanied the strong maternal
transference of the H.D.-Gregg sisterhood. H.D. found in Bryher a mutually nurturing mother/sister love who shared her
visions while allowing space for other loves, dreams, and imag-
inings. Bryher became the muse of "community" rather than
passionate introspection at a time when the related crises of war,
the loss of Josepha, and the dissolution of H.D.'s marriage ob-
sessed and paralyzed her art. H.D.'s Gregg had drawn her
inward toward "another country," where poetry and prophecy
were possible; the Bryher muse gave on to "open rock-hewn
wind-blown spaces of the intellect" (*Asphodel* 136). Both, however, harken back to the lost "sister love": at the conclusion of
Asphodel the Bryher figure's "blue eyes" call "to something in
Hermione that was lost . . . forgotten . . . taken away" (143).

The Bryher figure's late appearance in *Paint It Today, Asphodel,* or in short stories such as "Hipparchia" contrasts dramati-
cally with Fayne's or Josepha's hypnotic presence. While the
Gregg-figure suggests the fatal woman's combination of power
and danger, H.D.'s Bryher is more often a childlike figure from
the Greek past whose "chiseled" smallness the heroine records
with fascination and maternal tenderness. H.D.'s heroines are
less mesmerized but nonetheless in awe of these small, direct
women who repeatedly "save" them from isolation and despair.
In "Hipparchia," Moero (Bryher) resembles "some half-Asiatic
child-Hera" with "closely wrapped . . . coils of carefully braided
dark hair." White Althea in *Paint It Today* is "extremely pretty
. . . with eyes too intense for this generation, with bare feet too
perfect, with slight arms too delicate, for all their wiry play of
little nervous tendons" (71). The child-Bryher's "hard clarity"

both of appearance and approach immediately differs from the Gregg-figure's mysticism. Where Fayne was provocatively indirect, H.D.'s Bryher is disarmingly blunt. Hermione notes in *Asphodel* her "odd commanding look and . . . certainty" with admiration (and some alarm): "Hard face, child face . . . the smile froze across . . . the perfect white teeth" (118).

Finally, H.D.'s narrative of rebirth into a self-sustaining utopic community of women at the conclusion of *Paint It Today* encodes a mode of eros distinct from the mystic-erotic transport of "Faustine's" kiss in *HER*. Like the blissfully sensuous inhabitants of Vivien's Lesbos, Midget and White Althea thrive in the outdoor expanses of water and wood, reveling in the materiality of the body Midget calls "the visible world." Whereas the sexuality represented by Hermione and Fayne's "sessions" in Hermione's workroom converges to a point of intense focus where both women seem to "merge" in spiritual/emotional symbiosis, Althea and Midget's courtship ranges sensuously through winding waterway, storm-swept forest, and the warmth of a brazier-lit room. H.D.'s encoding of their sexual intimacy in the women's fierce battle with a stormy landscape emphasizes autonomy and release rather than fusion. "The daughters of Artemis's" erotic commune involves the diffuse, elemental play of the storm on "two" separate "alert and vivid bodies":

There was joy in them such as comes to the heart when certainty is upon us, after hours of tension and enervating unsatisfied expectancy.

Babies they were, girls or boys, with the wind about their bodies . . . half blinded with wind and slash of rain. . . . All the power of the wood seemed to circle between those two alert and vivid bodies, like two shafts attracting two opposite currents of the electric forces of the forest. (83, 84)

The narrative of "rescue" associated with Bryher in H.D.'s fiction of the twenties derives from actual dramatic events taking place in the first years of the women's intimacy. Both in their writing and in their personal lives, H.D. and Bryher mytholog-

ized their early union as having saved their lives. Bryher (Annie
Winifred Ellerman), who was twenty-four when she met the
thirty-two year old H.D. in 1918, was deeply despondent over
the strict social conventions that kept her at home with her
overpossessive mother and her father, a wealthy British shipping
magnate. She fell in love with H.D. "so madly it is terrible,"
H.D. wrote to John Cournos, and seriously threatened to com-
mit suicide if H.D. would not reciprocate. H.D., now pregnant
and worn down by war and the losses of Gregg and Aldington,
was initially reticent. According to H.D.'s account of the wom-
en's early intimacy in *Asphodel*, during one of her visits to the
rooms where H.D. was staying Bryher found the poet hovering
near death from influenza. After Bryher moved her to a nursing
home, the half-unconscious H.D. whispered to Bryher that if
she could visit her beloved Greece she would recover: "If I could
walk to Delphi, I should be healed." Bryher promised, "I will
take you to Greece as soon as you are well" (Guest 106). H.D.
recovered, bore a healthy child, and "gave" her daughter to
Bryher, who adopted the child, as a trust between them. A year
after Perdita was born, H.D. and Bryher traveled to Greece, the
imagined site of their meeting in *Asphodel, Paint It Today*, and
other works.

The changing complexity of H.D. and Bryher's long relationship, and the history of the several artistic, mythic, and "familial"
communities they would comprise in art and life, is beyond the
scope of this essay.[19] However, as Susan Friedman observes, "a
shared Artemisian discourse is more evident" in H.D. and Bryher's mythos of their relationship than in H.D. and Gregg's,
where, I have argued, the solitary femme fatale takes prece-
dence (*PW* 193). By the time H.D. had written the sequence of
chapters on Midget's meeting with "White Althea" in *Paint It
Today*, H.D., Perdita, and Bryher were already a family. The
concluding pages of the unfinished manuscript of *Paint It Today*
mention the miraculous "birth" that is to come, of a "creature"

who combines many colors of the "paint" indicated in the novel's
title, "white and black, amber and camellia white, [a creature]
not to be believed" (89). H.D.'s poems about Bryher and/or
Perdita often refer to communites of "two" or "three." In a poem
appropriately entitled "Triplex," H.D. celebrates her family of
women as "Greek" daughters of the goddess: "Let them grow
side by side in me,/ these three," . . . "Maid/ of the luminous
grey-eyes,/ Mistress of honey and marble white implacable thighs/
and Goddess,/ chaste daughter of Zeus/ most beautiful in the
skies" (CW 291).[20]

H.D.'s fascination with the femme fatale did not end, however, with the homoerotic novels of the 1920s. The later H.D.
appears to incorporate both "mother" muses represented by
Gregg and Bryher in the earlier homoerotic narratives. H.D.'s
long epic poems of the 1940s and 1950s, Trilogy and Helen in
Egypt, embrace the marginality and even the violence of the
Decadent female image, while, simultaneously, Trilogy's parade
of "dark" Venuses—Lilith, Mary of Magdella, and others—also
preside over an imagined "community" of a new "female" world
order. Seeking a muse with the leveling power to dismantle
patriarchal paradigms in her World War II mythos, H.D. turned
back to the transformative energy of the "terrible" mother-muse
she had regarded earlier with fear and suspicion.[21] In still another, coded configuration of female desire, Trilogy's narrator
addresses the erotic mother as both a "bitter" and transformative
distillation:

> sea, brine, breaker, seducer,
> giver of life, giver of tears;
>
> . . . .
> Star of the Sea
> Mother.
>
> (Trilogy 71)

Notes to the Introduction

The novel is published here exactly as H.D. wrote it. With the exception of typographical and grammatical corrections, and the transformation of British spelling and usage to its American counterpart, the text is presented in its original form.

1. *Asphodel* is forthcoming at Duke University Press in 1992. New Directions retitled H.D.'s novel *HERmione* because her original title, *HER*, overlapped with another publication. Here I refer to H.D.'s title, *HER*.
2. Susan Stanford Friedman is currently editing the H.D.-Bryher letters, which shed new light on the women's relationship and their place in the lesbian *milieu*.
3. I am indebted to Barbara Guest's biography of H.D., *HERself Defined: The Poet H.D.* for much of the biographical information in this essay. I am also indebted to Louis H. Silverstein's chronology, "Herself Delineated: Chronological Highlights of H.D."
4. H.D. was separated from Richard Aldington in 1918, although they were not divorced until 1938.
5. For important essays that specifically focus on H.D.'s lesbianism, see Susan Gubar's "Sapphistries"; Susan Stanford Friedman's and Rachel Blau DuPlessis's " 'I had Two Loves Separate': The Sexualities of H.D.'s *HER*"; Susan Friedman's recent ground-breaking book on H.D.'s prose, *Penelope's Web; Gender, Modernity and H.D.'s Prose,* which contains chapters on the lesbian narratives of *HER, Asphodel,* and *Paint It Today;* and my essay, "H.D. and A.C. Swinburne: Decadence and Modernist Women's Writing."
6. From Susan Friedman's interview with Sylvia Dobson (December 1990), reported in *Penelope's Web* (208).
7. Brigit Patmore's fictional account of the H.D.-Bryher-Aldington triangle in *No Tomorrow* in particular focuses on H.D.'s (and the narrator's) bisexuality. Patmore, who was in love with H.D. and who was among Aldington's adulterous attachments, was a less celebrated member of the London literary circle.
8. Friedman and DuPlessis make this point in "Two Loves" (216, 217).

9. For examinations of the search for the "mother" that underlies H.D.'s work and poetics, see Susan Friedman's *Psyche Reborn: The Emergence of H.D.*; Deborah Kelly Kloepfer's *The Unspeakable Mother: Forbidden Discourse in Jean Rhys and H.D.*; Rachel DuPlessis's discussion of *Trilogy* in *The Career of That Struggle*; and DuPlessis's essay, "Family, Sexes, and Psyche."

10. Karla Jay discusses Barney's and Vivien's "cult of the great mother," which they derived from Decadent Aestheticism, in chapter IV, "Sappho and Other Goddesses," of *The Amazon and the Page*. See also my essays, "H.D. and A.C. Swinburne," and "H.D.'s Romantic Landscapes: The Sexual Politics of the Garden."

11. Elyse Blankley points out this dichotomy in Vivien's poetry in her essays, "Return to Mytilene: Renée Vivien and the City of Women."

12. Elyse Blankley, Lillian Faderman, and Susan Gubar make this point.

13. I am suggesting that these diverse approaches to female sexuality, represented for instance by the "sado-masochism" of Monique Wittig's *Lesbian Body* and the mutual self-identifying sexuality of Rich's "Lesbian Continuum" in her much-quoted essay, should not be evaluated as "bad" or "good" or even as necessarily "opposed." They may be used to differentiate or articulate modes and levels of lesbian desire. By the same token, the image of the femme fatale need not be perceived exclusively as pornographic or misogynist. Nina Auerbach argues that the fatal woman informs an empowering "myth of womanhood" in Victorian literature and culture in *Woman and the Demon*. See also Gilbert's and Gubar's chapter 1, "Heart of Darkness: The Agon of the *Femme Fatale*," in volume 2 of *No Man's Land, Sexchanges*.

14. H.D. had read about Renée Vivien in an article, "A Pagan Poet," that appeared in the *Egoist* while she was assistant editor (1916–1917). She wrote enthusiastically to John Cournos, "Did you read the article in the *Egoist* about Renée Vivien? You must get Frank to tell you about her" (16 October 1918).

15. Apart from H.D.'s novels, versions of the refrain occur in the play *Hippolytus Temporizes* (53), in *End to Torment: A Memoir of Ezra Pound* (53), and in the long poem, *Helen in Egypt* (6, 107).

16. See Richard Dellamora's ground-breaking book, *Masculine Desire:*

The Sexual Politics of Victorian Aestheticism, for an in-depth exploration of the male homoerotic poetic in Victorian aesthetes such as Swinburne, Oscar Wilde, Walter Pater, and others.

17. Dellamora discusses the function and derivation of this particular code in Pater in chapter 5, "Arnold, Winckelmann, and Pater" (102–29) in *Masculine Desire.*

18. I discuss this passage in the context of the bisexual narrative of *HER* in "H.D. and A. C. Swinburne" (479).

19. H.D. and Bryher participated in a number of familial, artistic, and intellectual "communities." They formed at least two "ménages" with Bryher's husbands, Robert McAlmon and Kenneth Macpherson, the latter of whom H.D. fictionalized in her novels *Narthex* and *The Usual Star.* Bryher's influence also led to H.D.'s experience with avant-garde film and her analysis with Freud.

20. Adalaide Morris discusses the communal nature of H.D.'s visionary poetics in a number of essays. See especially her discussion of H.D.'s "gift economy" in "A Relay of Power and of Peace: H.D. and the Spirit of the Gift."

21. Susan Stanford Friedman argues in *Psyche Reborn* that H.D.'s analysis with Freud reconciled her both to her bisexuality and to the search for the mother that underlies her poetics—thus H.D. turned to the more "woman-centered" poetic of *Trilogy* and *Helen.* Deborah Kelly Kloepfer demonstrates that H.D. became reconciled to the "forbidden discourse" of the mother in her later poetry.

Works Cited

By H.D.

Asphodel. Beinecke Library, Yale University, New Haven, Conn. Forthcoming by Duke University Press, 1992.

Bid Me to Live (A Madrigal). Redding Ridge: Black Swan Books, 1983.

Collected Poems, 1912–1944. Edited by Louis L. Martz. New York: New Directions, 1983.

End to Torment: A Memoir of Ezra Pound. Edited by Norman Holmes Pearson and Michael King. New York: New Directions, 1979.

"Hipparchia." In *Palimpsest.* Carbondale: Southern Illinois University Press, 1968.

Hippolytus Temporizes. Boston: Houghton Mifflin, 1927.

HERmione. New York: New Directions, 1927.

"Murex." In *Palimpsest*. Carbondale: Southern Illinois University Press, 1968.

Narthex. The Second American Caravan: A Yearbook of American Literature. Edited by Alfred Kreymborg, Lewis Mumford, and Paul Rosenfeld. New York: Macaulay, 1928.

Paint It Today. First four chapters published in *Contemporary Literature* 27 (Winter 1986): 444–74. Complete manuscript at Beinecke Library, Yale University, New Haven, Conn.

Trilogy. New York: New Directions, 1973.

The Usual Star (and Two Americans). Dijon, France: Imprimèrie Darantière, 1934.

Other Works

Auerbach, Nina. *Woman and the Demon: The Life of a Victorian Myth*. Cambridge, Mass.: Harvard University Press, 1982.

Barnes, Djuna. *Ladies Almanack*. 1972. Reprint. New York: New York University Press, 1992.

Baudelaire, Charles. *Les Fleurs du Mal*. Paris, 1868.

Blankley, Elyse. "Return to Mytilene: Renée Vivien and the City of Women." In *Women Writers and the City*, edited by Susan Merrill Squier. Knoxville: University of Tennessee Press, 1984.

Cournos, John. *The Miranda Masters*. New York: Alfred A. Knopf, 1926.

Chodorow, Nancy. *The Reproduction of Mothering*. Berkeley: University of California Press, 1987.

Dellamora, Richard. *Masculine Desire: The Sexual Politics of Victorian Aestheticism*. Chapel Hill and London: University of North Carolina Press, 1990.

DuPlessis, Rachel Blau. *H.D.: The Career of That Struggle*. Bloomington: Indiana University Press, 1968.

———. "Family, Sexes, and Psyche: An Essay on H.D. and the Muse of the Woman Writer." *Montemora* 6 (1979).

———. "Romantic Thralldom in H.D." *Contemporary Literature* 20 no. 2 (Summer 1979).

Ellis, Havelock. "Sexual Inversion." In *Studies in The Psychology of Sex.* 4 vols. New York: Random House, 1936.

Faderman, Lillian. *Surpassing the Love of Men: Romantic Friendships and Love between Woman from the Renaissance to the Present.* New York: William Morrow, 1981.

Friedman, Susan Stanford. *Psyche Reborn: The Emergence of H.D.* Bloomington: Indiana University Press, 1981.

———. *Penelope's Web: Gender, Modernity, H.D.'s Fiction.* Cambridge: Cambridge University Press, 1990.

Friedman, Susan Stanford, and Rachel Blau DuPlessis, eds. " 'I had Two Loves Separate': The Sexualities of H.D.'s *HER.*" Reprinted in *Signets: Reading H.D.* Madison: University of Wisconsin Press, 1990.

Gubar, Susan. "Sapphistries." *Signs* 10, no. 1 (1984): 43–62.

Guest, Barbara. *HERself Defined: The Poet H.D. and Her World.* New York: Quill, 1984.

Hall, Radclyffe. *The Well of Loneliness.* 1928. Reprint. New York: Avon, 1980.

Jay, Karla. *The Amazon and the Page: Natalie Clifford Barney and Renée Vivien.* Bloomington: Indiana University Press, 1988.

Jay, Karla, and Joanne Glasgow, eds. *Lesbian Texts and Contexts: Radical Revisions.* New York: New York University Press, 1990.

Kloepfer, Deborah Kelly. *The Unspeakable Mother: Forbidden Discourse in Jean Rhys and H.D.* Ithaca and London: Cornell University Press, 1989.

Laity, Cassandra. "H.D. and A.C. Swinburne: Decadence and Modernist Women's Writing." *Feminist Studies* 15, no. 3 (Fall 1989): 461–84. Reprinted in *Lesbian Texts and Contexts,* 217–40.

———. "H.D.'s Romantic Landscapes: The Sexual Politics of the Garden." *Sagetrieb* 6, no. 2 (Fall 1987): 57–75. Reprinted in *Signets: Reading H.D.,* 110–28.

Lindenbaum, Joyce P. "The Shattering of an Illusion: The Problem of Competition in Lesbian Relationships." *Feminist Studies* 11, no. 1 (Spring 1985): 85–103.

Morris, Adalaide. "A Relay of Power and of Peace: H.D. and the Spirit of the Gift." *Contemporary Literature* 27 (Winter 1986).

———. "Signaling: Feminism, Politics and Mysticism in H.D.'s War Trilogy." Paper read at King's College, Cambridge, U.K., Summer 1991.

Patmore, Brigit. *No Tomorrow*. New York: Century Company, 1929.

Rich, Adrienne. "Compulsory Heterosexuality and Lesbian Existence." *Signs* 5, no. 4 (1980): 631–60.

Silverstein, Louis H. "Herself Delineated: Chronological Highlights of H.D." In *Signets: Reading H.D.*, edited by Susan Stanford Friedman and Rachel Blau DuPlessis. Madison: University of Wisconsin Press, 1990.

Stimpson, Catharine. "Zero Degree Deviancy: The Lesbian Novel in English." In *Writing and Sexual Difference*, edited by Elizabeth Abel, 243–59. Chicago: University of Chicago Press, 1982.

Swinburne, A. C. *The Complete Works*. Vol. 1, edited by Sir Edmund Gosse and Thomas Hames Wise. London: Heinemann, 1925.

Vivien, Renée. *A Woman Appeared to Me*. Introduction by Gayle Rubin. Translated by Jeannette H. Foster. Tallahassee, Fla. Naiad Press, 1979.

Wittig, Monique. *The Lesbian Body*. Translated by David Le Vay. Boston: Beacon, 1986.

PAINT IT TODAY

ONE

Morning and Evening Star

A PORTRAIT, a painting? You cannot paint today as you painted yesterday. You cannot paint tomorrow as you paint today. A portrait, a painting? Do not paint it of yesterday's rapt and rigid formula nor of yesterday's day-after-tomorrow's criss-cross—jagged, geometric, prismatic. Do not paint yesterday's day-after-tomorrow destructiveness nor yesterday's fair convention. But how and as you will—*paint it today.*

A portrait, a painting? There are white pear trees and a wysteria's knotted vine stock, untidy with its rope-colored strands of fibrous, tattered bark, fraying from the wood. The wysteria, long embedded in the undershingles of the low roof, has thrown its blossoms this year far out of reach, into the branches of the nearest pear.

The pear is an English Bartlett grafted with a French cuisse-madame. The two grafts are distinct in their blossoming and the wysteria smothers both down like a vine with ghosts of clusters, the pale blue upper petals of each separate flower from a cap over the lower horns of violet.

The child itself, I would make dark cypress wood, rounded

head, clawlike hands, an archaic, small Hermione,[1] a nameless, foundling sister of Princess Minnehaha, a bird or intermediate, of a lost reptile race, clawing its way into the pear and wisteria tangle, to cling, to be lost, to defy worlds from there, to crack the sky with an ugly, screwed-up little face, screwed up into the blaze of ozone, spring air, air forged, whetted of ice on wind.

A portrait? Paint it yesterday on porcelain, in print pinafore and leghorn wreathed with cornflowers. Paint it today; colt knees crawling into the rabbit hutch, scent of old straw and this morning's lettuce leaves and yesterday's half-gnawed carrot tops and sprinklings of oats and stiff straws to print little, half-perceived pricklings on the grimed knees and length of half-leg. Crawling, crawling with elbows scraping the rough lathes and a loose end of wire netting to tangle in the short, stubbly rough hair, to be rewarded at the last with a vision of eight pink bodies, eight unexpectedly furless and rigid bodies, to be lifted, one by one from the nest of tight packed straw, and cherished against a quivering cheek, to be pressed, breathed on, and to be replaced, this ferret's quarry, in the nest, while the weary old bunny thumps, disconsolate in the corner.

Paint her portrait; she is sitting in the grass, this Midget. She is playing with the Edwards's children, of whom, not inappropriately, there are eight. The two oldest are, by one year and two years, older than this Midget. They are wonderful and goddesslike, the one, almost out of reach, with long, thick plaits, is called Olive; the next, beautifully and graciously condescending to this Midget is Cornelia. She has black hair, a mop, which just escapes her shoulders.

The rest of the Edwards's children, a graduated scale, one more girl, then five boys, melt into the background of the commonplace. Olive and Cornelia, like a young Hera and Artemis,[2] the one mothering, the other championing in games and hunts and expeditions, dominate for a space, the spirit of this Midget, who with stiff legs and arms and short hair and no grace and beauty of girlhood seems of an inferior race, perhaps a minute demi-god or hero beside these beings, capable and efficient and alert to men and women and the manners of the world. Yet, though it is true that Cornelia found the mulberry tree, and Olive headed the trail of multiplying Edwardses and stray neighbors' children, to the deserted garden, it was Midget who scaled the tree, who shook the branches in a frenzy, till the multiplying Edwardses were drenched in the soft, too-ripe, purple blackberries which yet tasted so unlike blackberries, mellow, oversweetened yet not sweet.

Her portrait? Find her on the trail of the Pennsylvania foothills breaking her first bunches of the wax-pink mountain laurel; find her with a screwed-up knot of precious wild arbutus, or the first wandlike bough of dogwood. Find her, differentiate her, carve her from dark cypress wood, only to lose her again, her valiant outline blurred in the process of civilizing, of schooling, of devitalizing.

There is a brave scholar, a thing of hunched shoulders and sparrow claws, who with unabated intensity, scratched 7, 7, 7, 7, 7 across the entire length of great sheets of brown wrapping paper, spread on the nursery floor. A small line, flat with the top of the paper, joined to a line, longer yet, of possibly varying lengths, stood for something more potent, more cabalistic than the two marks of equal length joined, tentwise, and fastened across the middle. An A was a flat, formless, unsuggestive figure. But the 7 could be done in different colored chalks forever across great sheets of paper. Oh stop, stop, stop, parents, schoolteachers, professors, horde of the unredeemed. Is there no law to stand between you and the perfected? Is there no new lawmaker to arise and damn you to a yet unthinkable perdition?

Yet a beautiful thing, a perfect thing is inevitably broken. The small bird, fallen from its nest was so hideous, so wormlike with a repellent gruesomeness the smooth, clean, snakelike angle-worms or the flat garden grubs never had. The egg was so pretty with flecks of brown and vermilion on its Nile-green shell. The small bird was an uncanny monster. Perhaps the Midgets of this world would become curious, misshapen things if they were not captured early. What is the use of mourning for the broken egg shell when there is some hope in a small monster of flight or gift of singing?

I find it a cold and perhaps thin and lifeless picture, this etching of a spirit. Yet I must make an etching or an economized wood carving or a faintly tinted quattrocento fresco, as this is, at the moment, the only possible way that I can work. I know that the important things in the tempering of a soul are perhaps the rough, the commonplace, that seem to youth and early maturity unimportant, stifling, even inhibiting surroundings or conditions. But at the moment, I am attempting, not so much, to reproduce an atmosphere, a medley of conditions and circumstances and surroundings, and to show how a single being pierced through them, or slung its tenuous way across them (the invisible, glistening thread, that counts for intuition and valor in the darkness of the impenetrable forest). I am trying rather to give a picture of that being, that spider, that small, hatched bird, that flawless shell that once contained an unborn being.

The conditions and surroundings of its youth are much the conditions of most of the children of the comfortable, not too well-to-do members of the middle or so-called professional classes. The chief hunger of this particular child's childhood was not hunger for food or sleep or fires or the little festivities of babyhood. I think, as the only girl in a very large family, she wanted most passionately a girl child of her own age, a twin sister, which, in the frantic, premature passion that comes to many children at about the age of ten, she visualized poignantly and with curious desperate yearning as a very little sister, a baby sister.

This particular yearning for one child, a girl of its own particular temperament, was satisfied when Midget had left school, had left childhood, girlhood; was drifting unsatisfied, hurt and baffled out of a relationship with a hectic, adolescent, blundering, untried, mischievous, and irreverent male youth.[3] When she was nineteen, she had parted with the youth, having gained nothing from him but a feeling that someone had tampered with an oracle, had banged on a temple door, had dragged out small curious, sacred ornaments, had not understood their inner meaning, yet with a slight sense of their outer value, their perfect tint and carving, had not stolen them, but left them, perhaps worse, exposed by the roadside, reft from the shelter and their holy setting.

She was desperate and tired and weary in her very early twenties. What chemistry and the binomial theorem had not drained from her of avidity and living fervor, the male adolescent had. She had not the strength nor courage to snap fresh and vivid from the surroundings of her childhood. She had no sap or vivid living power left in her. She felt instinctively that she was a failure by all the conventional and scholarly standards. She had failed in her college career,[4] she had failed as a social asset with her family and the indiscriminate mob of relatives and relays of communal friends that surrounded it. She had burned her candle of rebellion at both ends and she was left unequipped for the simplest dealings with the world.

Into this weariness, into this morass of inhibitions, of failures, of cramped brain and body, there came as to Paul of Tarsus,[5] light.

The light, as I believe frequently happens in these circumstances, came from the most unexpected quarter. She had been invited by one of the usual hangers-over of tepid school friendships, to an "afternoon." There was nothing to be done about it.

Midget, held to the framework of the indiscriminate middle-class society she moved in, too listless to rebel actually from it, was yet too listless, at the particular moment, to frame an adequate excuse and went.

She dawdled away an hour over ices and macaroons, wondering why she had come. Then she knew why she had come.

It was not that the girl Josepha,[6] was beautiful, judged by the ordinary standards. She came into the room, stood stiff against the oak doors that closed heavily behind her. She was inordinately self-conscious. Perhaps she was shy.

The girl Mary, relic of the tepid school, rose to meet her.

The girl Midget went on talking to two stupid creatures, not girls, not women, from an art school.

She watched the other or listened to the other, whichever it could be called, out of the two veins, throbbing, midway between the space joining eye and ear.

The other sat down. She had on a raincoat that fitted closely and a stiff straw hat wound with a stiff gray veil. This gave her an old fashioned appearance, a distinction in this room filled with the daughters of lawyers, doctors, professors, and oversuccessful wholesale merchants.

Mary the relic had always been noted for her soft voice, her chosen speech, her very exquisite assumption that the scholarship girls in the special classes were, after all, in the gracious and kingly republic she dwelled in, not to be ignored. Then too occasionally these scholarship girls had been known to succeed in the world. One made her musical debut in Vienna. One had been well spoken of by a London art critic. Anyway, the kingly republic had created all men equal.

Mary was purring with her chosen voice, the voice that was inevitably known to put scholarship girls at ease, that purred away the jagged corners of social inequality. She was asking something of the other girl about her work.

The other girl's face was slightly spotted. Her color was bad. The slate gray raincoat did not do it justice. The gray veil was not altogether an inspiration. The girl (Midget thought) somehow or other felt this, was almost glad of this.

It was her eyes, set in the unwholesome face; it was the shoulders, a marble splendor, unspoiled by the severe draping of straight cut rainproof; it was her hand, small, unbending, stiff with archaic grandeur; it was her eyes, an unholy splendor.

Her eyes were the blue eyes it is said one sees in heaven; eyes, Angelo would have garnered in a group of holy boys, copied for one face and re-created for another; eyes a Messalina[7] might have wrought (to stab a Caesar) into bright steel; eyes the color of wet hyacinths before the spikes have broken into flower.

The eyes rested now on Midget. The nose, puckered into two tiny wrinkles, just outlined the upper curve of nostril. The mouth turned ever so slightly downward at the corners.

The voice, like Mary's, was gentle and attuned. It too ignored all social inequality. The blue eyes rested on the gray eyes, devouring like a storm that space of uttermost and bluest heaven. The voice spoke: "Ah, you too, Miss Defreddie, are you too interested in college settlements?"

It may have been true, as the family stated, that the girl Josepha was not a good influence, had an unwholesome quality about her somehow, was not normal, was not quite the friend they would have chosen, at least not the friend to the exclusion of other friends they would have chosen. The young erstwhile fiancé, now on formal terms and friendly with the family circle, may also have been right when he twitched his very young mustaches and thrust out his slightly underdeveloped chin and said: "You and that girl, a hundred years ago, would have been burned at Salem, for witches."

The hounds of Hecate[8] might have dogged Josepha's footprints. She loved green things, the sound of water, the chaste, untouched, the gold and frozen daffodils too much. She was undoubtedly unwholesome. She knew no Latin. Midget, who forgave everything, for some inexplicable reason could not forgive her this.

Tomorrow, ah tomorrow, let us love. We who love now, let us go on loving all day, all day tomorrow. Let us who have never loved, love tomorrow. Let us love tomorrow. Twist it how you will, go on twisting it, repeating and recalling the white echoes with the glint of swift tomorrows; it is no use, it is no good at all.

Cras amet[9]—

The worlds had broken down, all the worlds, at least all the reasonable and reasoning worlds filled with all the people of reason, parents, every friend, the shadow of the erstwhile fiancé, who had guessed at something but who had never penetrated beyond the worlds of today. Today. It had always been today. Today had been a small pebble, marked with moss patterns, as pretty as the lark's egg; today had been a larger, small stone, curved prettily; today had become delightful and suggestive blocks of small unhewn marble; today had been today. And all the time, today was forging its millstone out of childhood, and girlhood, and very young womanhood, till it hung with the affections of the past, a tyranny, a slave yoke about her neck.

—qui numquam amavit[10]—

You who have never loved. That was translatable enough. No one had ever loved. No one she knew had known what love was or could be. Love was a creature of the senses. Love was not the touching of hands, the meeting of lips. Love had nothing to do with the circumstances of your birth, or the conditions of your life.

The girl Josepha was, no doubt, an unwholesome influence. It would have been much better if the girl Midget had married the fiancé.

Poetry and the beat and drop of poetry, the swerve up and the swallow wing[11] beating back. The girl Midget had chosen

her poetry out of the mass and the tumult of the world's poetry
(as far as her mind could follow it) carefully.

> I have come again away from the dead,
> Drawn by strange powers to thee,
> Quicken me now nor fear to give,
> Too much of yourself to me. [12]

She had translated it painstakingly from Heine, and she knew
that she had brought over a little the fragrance of the German.
She worried about the "thee" and the "yourself" but "thyself"
sounded stilted, unnatural.

Poetry and the beat and the swallow wings. Large, epic pictures bored her, though she struggled through them. She wanted
the songs that cut like a swallow wing the high, untainted ether,
not the tragic legions of set lines that fell like black armies with
terrific force and mechanical set action, paralyzing, or broke like
a black sea to baffle and to crush.

> "I have come again away from the dead."

How many times did they come from the dead?

The dead? Surely that was yesterday but it seemed tomorrow.
The dead? Was it not today and all that today contained of
friends and relatives and the shadow of the understanding that
the fiancé had given her that she was dead? Which was dead and
which was living. Vaguely, she had of late years asked herself
this. Now she set herself the task, like a problem in arithmetic,
of answering the question not vaguely, groping into psychic
layers of fog and probabilities, but sternly, with the emotions, it
is true, but the emotions of the sculptor rather than of the
musician.

The dead?

> —*quique amavit* [13]—

Whoever has loved. Whoever, whoever has loved. Has loved.
In all the past has loved. Who was it that had loved? Heine had

loved and it had drawn him from the dead. Plato had loved and it had drawn him to the star in the end, among the living. Thou wert the morning star among the living.

> Thou wert the morning star among the living,
> Ere thy fair light was shed,
> Now having died thou art as Hesperus giving
> New splendor to the dead. [14]

Hesperus. That was the evening star. The morning star. The morning stars sang together. Among the living. That was neither past nor future, it was past and future together. It was a state containing past and future.

When she and Josepha, after the inevitable preliminary ramblings together in the present, the present which was dead, found themselves for the first time face to face, the present which was dead melted away and they were together in the past and in the future. They spoke very few words. They hardly touched each other's hands. They spoke a few words, at least it was Midget who spoke the words.

Midget knew that she was speaking simple words and understandable words. She understood them herself and Josepha understood them, but she felt somehow that she was speaking the wrong language. She was speaking English.

The past and the future, morning and evening star, hung there, a beacon in the darkness between this world and the future, the present and the future. She had, through the clarity of her youth, through the intensity of her passion, and through that fate or chance that had thrown her in Josepha's way at a curious psychological moment (at the moment when she had been touched by the shadow of an understanding, stirred by it, but not awakened), surprised a curious secret, surprised the secret or found the door to another world, another state of emotional life or being, a life of being that contained the past and the future. Morning and evening star had met and swayed a

second in the high air above the earth, morning and evening star
had met and sung together. But it was a tenuous though all so
clarid singing. It was the overnote of the tortured violin, the
echo of the seashell. Midget, though the secret was to color all
her life, was yet unsatisfied. She must find a link between the
morning and the evening star (though she spent her life in
seeking), and the earth she trod on.

TWO

Below Etaples

THE wind against an old hulk on the sands below Etaples, was not yet wind, not wind that is when contrasted with that rush of swords that cut the sand stretches into snow and ice patterns and blared through the Maine pines and tore in midsummer, tornadowise, walnut and tough oak branches from the walnut and great oak trees. Wind as they had known wind was an assailing tyrant, bringing not only its own self, a physical and robust being to be dealt with physically and with what strength they had, but bringing too, like an unwary, indiscreet and untaught lover, scent of its mistress's hair and eyelids, steeped in orchid. Was that it? Was that quite how they felt it? Yes, these Europeans could not know. They appreciated somehow the roughness and the power of that wilderness Josepha and Midget had left, wildly exultant in this their first trip to Europe, but did they know, could they guess at that other force, hidden and hardly guessed at by these others, transplanted Europeans, called Americans? If these Americans could not sense the fine trail winding through their midst, could these others, these Europeans, be expected to recognize it?

Yet what they had lost in the sting and dash of spray, in the rains and wind, they gained elsewhere. Continually on the watch and alert to minute signs, even in the seemingly common place, of the foreign, the picturesque, the quaint, the un-American, today their attention was focused on the old hulk, blown windward, half filled with heavy, earthlike sand. It was the letters, scratched across its bow that most inflamed their imaginations. The name was half obliterated. The letters, cut with a slightly Gothic twist, might have stood for an Andros, or Arcadia or Helenis [15] stranded there from southern waters. They had really not touched the south here. Yet they saw in the sifted evening light that caught the surface of a sea pool far up on the flat beach a suggestion of some holy inland lake. At least, it was Josepha who said it made her think of a scene from Galilee.

The sun was going down. Yet this was not the sun, this flameless, low-swinging, mid-European substitute.

The sunset gave them a smothered, lifeless feeling; the sun was not a sun, yet these people trailing up from the sands were people, authentic people, as the same trailing herd, dark colored, grouped in shapeless knots on the dazzling Atlantic shore, were hardly to be identified, singled out one from another as separate human beings. Yet there was a big young girl in a bunched-up skirt, too tall, regarded from American standards, to swing along with a little girl's spade and painted bucket. A big girl, yet evidently by European standards still a child, an individual anyway and her companion an individual, with individual and fashionable clothes, yet a child too with her great wide-brimmed dark blue hat. The little boy following was a social unit and a decorative unit in his French-red matelot. These and others, trailing in leisurely procession, were surely people, authentic realities (as authentic as paper dolls, cut out front and back, matched front and back), each a reality, an individual, conventionalized, as real as paper dolls, differentiated.

That was it, she and Josepha argued, the background, flat, low, small, drab, a little brought them out, gave them proportion, as the dark gray vine scroll on the gray carpet gave the paper dolls a house, a garden, a driveway to a house.

There was no carpet beneath the feet of the Americans. The blaze on the New Jersey sands burned reality from them. Almost Midget and Josepha could imagine they saw right through them; the people seemed only a blur, smearing the white plains of sand.

Here in France, at Etaples, the people were a reality. In America, it was the white sand that lived, the wind, the stainless rout of stars.

And in America she and Josepha lived; by some defeatless law of compensation, such as she and Josepha lived in America.

In a little museum at Havre, they had blown against a wall, and Midget saw that Josepha's eyes had gone a new gray, a different gray.

Julia (Josepha's mother) was trailing with a catalog from picture to picture. Her eyes were on the pictures, but she was watching Josepha, watching Midget. Sometimes Julia and Midget snarled, tore at one another as Midget had never snarled, nor been snarled at in her life. Sometimes Midget forgot that she must watch, watch always between Josepha and Julia, and she would be almost of an age with Julia, joined together suddenly, forgetting everything in an ecstasy of discovery that Josepha's eyes had gone a new color.

Josepha had wound the gray veil across her small, stiff straw. She was wearing the jacket of her little, gray traveling dress although it was too warm, and she had found a chair in the corner of the gallery when Midget came on her.

So intense was Midget's exclamation at the new color of Josepha's eyes, that Julia, ever present and ever vigilant governess, turned suddenly.

They argued in friendly enmity: "She has taken the tone from the spattered rock and gray and lump-of-paint rocks of the Monet opposite."

"It was only the gray veil that did it."

"It was the way she was facing the daylight, sifting across the jetties of the Havre backwater."

"It was nothing at all; it was the usual way Josepha's eyes went."

But Josepha's eyes had never done that before, though they had been carefully observed in the woods, beneath the variously diffusing greens of beach and fir, and in all the changes of the sea, in the stormy days and when the tide stream met them, mid-Atlantic, with tufts of exotic weed and great, uprearing dolphins.

Paint it today. Aye, there is an easy maxim. Midget, turning back pages, looked at the words.

She, Midget, did not wish to be an eastern flower painter. She did not wish to be an exact and over-*précieuse* western, a scientific describer of detail of vein and leaf of flowers, dead or living, nor did she wish to press flowers and fern fronds and threads of pink and purple seaweed between the pages of her book. Yet she wanted to combine all these qualities in her writing and to add still another quality to these three. She wished to embody, as this other quality, the fragrance of the flowers.

You cannot paint fragrance, you cannot be a sculptor of fragrance, you cannot play fragrance on a violin. Yet you can, with a pencil, at least attempt to express something in definite terms, before which the violin, the chisel, and the brush are powerless.

She remembered her surprise at hearing in a London drawing room a sophisticated, well-bred woman say: "Ah, just back from the south of France. He says his vineyards are in blossom. I had never thought of the flowering of vines, had you?" Fluttering toward her neighbor: "He says he will have a house party and invite me especially next spring. It is indescribable, he says"

. . . , and she went on pattering prettily, describing the indescribable as descriptively described to her.

Again it came to her as it had come many times in these London drawing rooms, what centuries they were apart, centuries in time, centuries in space. Did they live in the same world? She and Josepha (and such as she and Josepha) lived isolated, clarid, separate, distinctive lives in America. That was natural. It was natural that she and Josepha and such as she and Josepha should be cast out of the mass of the living, out of the living body, as useless as natural wastage, excrementitious, it is true, thrown out of the mass, projected forth, crystallized out, orient pearls, to stand forever after, a reflection somehow, on the original rasped and wounded parent.

That was a formal process. That was a process of nature. America, the universally accepted smeltering place of nations, raised to a higher level, through its genial temperament and generous educational ventures, the lower strata of the mediocrities, drew down to its mediocre strata those just above its middle level, evening off, evening off, continually reducing to the golden commonplace, the dead and comfortable and quiet level. The golden, comfortable commonplace drew to it and comforted those not too uncomfortable, drew to its humanitarian heart the frore and higher intellect and brain that yet conformed to its highest ideal of shape and pattern. Midget, outwardly standardized by early environment, was not too disconcerting to the rabble. Josepha, through prenatal accident and the shocks attending a precarious childhood, had learned early to distrust them. She was, in turn, more or less avoided by them. Her eyes discountenanced them.

It was the same in London. They regarded Josepha as someone different; in their studios, perhaps someone "interesting," to be dealt with later. They looked at Midget, tall to the breaking-in-the-middle point, with fluttering hat brim and tenuous ankles, as of their own world, too young to be noticed or to be regarded suddenly with a jerk in the midst of pleasant, normal conversation, suddenly on guard as if, unwittingly, they had betrayed themselves. "What *you*, an American?"

You, an American; yes, she was an American. In time, in space, a thousand, thousand years separated from this English woman, pretty, civilized, of her own world, sympathetic, well dressed, who was pattering of grape blossoms and a house party in the south of France.

Not because she was pattering rubbish was she these thousand years separated from a Midget who could patter rubbish with the best. Nor was it exactly because she, Midget, distinctly recollected at about the age of four a special day, when she herself became initiated, suddenly alert and taut, in one of her frenzies of exploration. She was crawling under the wood framework of the arbor, crushing with lithe shoulders and small body, the narrow border of green spikes, now a little wilted, no more to be respected, mere coarse, unshorn grass, since the small globes of flower drops had melted out from the leaf tufts in the new heat; a new layer of heat, a distinctly different layer. This special midspring heat layer was to be forever after associated in Midget's mind with a new fragrance which (sprawling under the lathes of the grape arbor, with the heat of this new consistency distinctly a pressure on her back, with the memory of the snowdrops, the flowers themselves, and the snow itself, so subtly disappearing yet merging with the memory of those first flowers) could only be described as *cold*. This cold fragrance was soon identified with the tiny green feather bunches curling out from the very young, very small underfurred, red-tipped leaves of the grapevine. This was the fragrance of the grape flowers, if flowers these young spikes, resembling the unripe lilac blossoms, could be called.

It was no fault of this English woman, pretty, sophisticated, that she had never felt or smelled or tasted grapevines flowering. It was no fault of her English friend in France that he burbled rot about them. Both of these people were manifestly inexpert in their dealings with the finer matters of the senses. Also, they were manifestly insincere. Yet this insincerity, or rather triviality, toward matters of (to her) the gravest import she soon learned that they regarded as if not exactly a virtue, at least as one of the (if not one of the most important) earmarks of social caste. Americans especially were gently and whimsically derided now and again in her presence for intensity or earnestness. She, insinuated in their midst, tall and shy in the manner of their own people, would feel suddenly an imposter, almost an eavesdropper. Was it better to blurt forth that there was a stranger at the gates or to sink further and shyer into the soft recesses of the chintz-covered chesterfield?

She and Josepha and such as she and Josepha were separated, irreparably, from the masses of their own country people. That was natural, stoically to be regarded as a process of nature. But it came as a shock to find that they were separated not only from the masses but also from the refined, the sensuous, the artistically differentiated as well. They had a special quality of their own. There was no use saying that American women were more like French women. It meant nothing and it was not true. Somehow, they had imagined, speaking the same language, bred in the same tradition, that in London they would find their own. It was not so.

Language and tradition do not make a people, but the heat that presses on them, the cold that baffles them, the alternating lengths of night and day.

She and Josepha were separated, and such as she and Josepha were separated from the great mass of the people of the nations of the world. They were separated from the separated too; how can we make that clear? They were separated from the elite, from the artist, the musician, at least from all the artists and literary specimens it had been their privilege so far to encounter, in the art circles of the midlayers of so-called Bohemia.

It was something in themselves. Josepha knew all about it. She said quite clearly, "So and so hates me; so and so sees that I see." Midget did not know anything about it. She moved shyly with a sort of immature school girl sincerity that made people think her younger than she was and sheltered and perhaps just a little shallow.

Josepha knew all about it. She had grown up an only child, watched and pampered by Julia. She had learned early to lie to Julia. When she was a baby she had danced for Julia and Julia's mother, while, Julia (too, an only child) played little songs. Julia's mother watched Julia and watched Josepha intensely. It might have been said that Julia had never really grown up.

They had something in common, these three, Julia, Josepha, and Midget. I think most probably, at a casual venture, you would have said it was their eyes. Perhaps that it was, too, that might have made one think, if a color could have played about them, that color would have been, emphatically, blue. Their eyes were very different, yet they were all blue eyes, eyes static in their blue, you would have said, as stars, and if you watched long enough you would have found that Julia's did stay blue; though Josepha's eyes would change suddenly and altogether, from blue to slate gray, or a rain gray but always a definite color; while Midget's eyes would change indefinitely, like blue and cold waves washing intermediately, separating, yet always flowing one into the other, the sky blue of the water and the cold.

There was a clash in them of mixed race, yet in general effect, though they as individuals were so different, it was the same mixture. Julia had come of an old Dutch family with intermixture of more common English. Josepha's father had been Scotch. Midget was a more vivid clash of north or almost Norse English and the very southern Polish or Lithuanian German.

I have stated before that they were all Americans.

THREE

Cras Amet

Cras amet qui numquam amavit,
quique amavit, cras amet.

TOMORROW, let him love who never has guessed the meaning of love; whoever has loved, or in some way apprehended what love might be or become, let him love, let him love tomorrow.

The fiancé had shown Midget what love might be or become if one, in desperation, should accept the shadow of an understanding for an understanding itself. Josepha had shown her or she had shown Josepha what love was or could be or become if the earth, by some incautious legerdemain, should be swept from beneath our feet; and we were left ungravitated between the stars.

I do not wish to belittle the Josepha incident. It colored Midget's life; it colors it still.

But there are many colors to our lives, I have been led to believe. The shadow of an understanding is not a bad beginning to one's emotional radius. Against the shadow, the better things

22

show true. But the truth of Josepha was too amazing a truth. The blue of the rainbow must not dazzle out the rose and yellow and primrose yellow and violet and dark purple. There is perhaps one truth which even the rainbow must put up with and that is the emotional white truth. That came later to our Midget, long past the compass of this story. It might be added that a black truth accompanied it, a truth beside which the shadow of the fiancé's misunderstanding was but the shadow, the very small and watered shadow, of a shadow. It might be added, but I never quite believed it. At least, it seemed to me when I had time to think it over, that a shadow (black enough) becomes a glorious color, not a glorious color but the heart of a glorious color, like the innermost heart of the intense anemone, or like the fervor of dark eyes.

But we have not yet reached the fervor of dark eyes and our setting is blue. Here we have power to choose, we magicians, we failures, we ourselves, our very selves, poets and lovers. Although in a sense, we have not chosen this blue scene, it has rather chosen us.

But it has not chosen us, we have chosen (if we have chosen) to become spectators of it. But it chose for a moment, for a second of a heartbeat, Midget and Josepha to become part of it.

The columns of Hadrian's country villa at Tivoli beyond Rome have, as is customary with the columns of the country villas of the great, toppled down. I have walked through long woods, off the main road beyond Frascati, on marble paving stones, wide enough, it was stated, for a pair of oxen, though personally I thought the oxen must be very thin ones. The path is too wide, however, for a person, especially if the person is intoxicated with the feel of paving stones in the heart of a great forest. If the person is an American and has known intimately the hearts of many forests, this feeling of paving stones under his shoes is sure to violently upset him. In his upset condition, he wobbles from side to side, he feels that the stones are a marble bridge, built

across this immensity of green water. He feels with all his wob-
bling that he must not, dare not slide off the paving stones into
the green water.

Some Americans get drunk this way. I doubt if many Europeans do.

And why should Europeans get drunk? In Paris in some
impossible Montmartre area or in some place quite in the opposite direction, there is a small and pretty theater, built in the
year about 200, with all urbanity, with correct and nicely graded
little rows of benches. I doubt if any Parisian has ever been
there, but I went. It was very hot and horses were munching
lupin sort of grass and small boys were hurling filth at one
another. Why should any European get drunk at the sight of a
paving stone? Even in London, though I never tracked it out,
there are authentic mosaics, looking very fresh, I am sure, and
in very bad taste, side by side with the more than Roman
standardized stability of the paving stones themselves.

But to return to the forest beyond Frascati. The person (who
was, more or less, myself) stopped dead at a curve in the road.
A small altar was set under a larch tree. There was no particular
reason to believe that it was not there.

If I had been told that it was not there, no doubt I would have
believed what I was told. But my companion,[16] who was young
and sympathetic, and English, murmured something in Latin.
The Latin being English Latin, I did not altogether follow, but I
gleaned something about Pan and a sheath of some garb or other
and an offering.

I was very glad at that time, for my companion, as his voice
was not American. He let me think without interrupting what I
was thinking and he had just enough sense to know when I was
thinking. He flattered me, too in his charming way. He told me
very often that I spoke English better than any American he had
ever known or any Englishman.

He was not a bit annoyed when I sat on the paving stones.

He was tolerant and kind. He told me that the small, under-sized white and yellow crocuses jabbing now out of the black wood mold where the sun fell through the sparser young spring foliage were called saffron.

Myself, who was an unformed sort of nebulous personality at the time of the wanderings round Frascati, shall have no name. People called me Miss Defreddie, which was surely not a name, or if it was a name it was a thing to be laughed at. If people laughed I was embarrassed and tried to laugh with them as if I had never heard just that laugh at just that particular name before. If they did not laugh, it was equally embarrassing, because one wondered if they had not heard properly, or if they were concealing the laugh and would suddenly burst forth with it like someone who has inadvertently swallowed a bit of hot potato. There are all kinds of people and all kinds of feigned indifference and subterfugings and escapings from the joke. The best people are undoubtedly the French, who really thought it was a *de* and were very courteous. There were also English people who seemed pleased and said, "How charming, how quaint."

Myself who was an unformed sort of nebulous personality shall have no name. You might have called me Midget if you were very stupid, but I was not Midget. Midget was an intense star, Midget was a reality. Midget had broken from all humanity, had fought and won, was a flaming banner. Josepha had called her a white sword flower.

But if you had looked carefully, you would have seen there was no sword in my face. Possibly if you had looked again, you would have realized it was in my heart.

I was to have told a story or set a scene of a blue world. I will tell it in my own time, in my own way. Whoever has loved, let him love. Let him love today assuredly of his own will and let him love tomorrow, alas, no longer of his own volition. Let him love today because his hands are cold or because he wants someone who will understand with him, or counterargue with him, the evolved and insoluble political situation. Let him love today because his hands are cold. Tomorrow he will no longer be able to choose the creature of his loving.

Rome and the outposts of Rome set against the whole world! Somewhere in one of those outlying painted cities there had once been a Josepha, there had once been a Midget. What they had been, flower girls, or prostitutes, or captured slaves or page boys or young scribes, or one a scribe and one a butcher's daughter, I can never tell you. Rome and the outposts of Rome. That runs in my head, *arma virumque*, that beats down the battered fortress of my brain, *cano*.[17] I sing of arms and a god. Rome and the Tuscan foothills.

What do I sing? I don't know what I sing. What anyhow does it matter what I sing, I, a nebulous personality without a name.

But I will not let *I* creep into this story. I will not let *I* go on banging the tinkling cymbal of its own emotion. You and I are out of this story, are observing and (if you will let *I* still intrude by way of speaking out opinions) I think, myself, that Midget really was a lucky girl.

Midget that lucky girl, although she had only bargained with her parents for the four months summer holiday abroad with Josepha and Mrs. McAlpin, found letters awaiting her at the American Express, Haymarket, in London, on their arrival there from France late in August, stating that owing to certain tedious family matters, unexpectedly settled, Professor and Mrs. Defreddie were about to cross to Genoa in November. So Midget need not return as planned with the McAlpins. She could stay in London with approved old Anglo-American acquaintances and meet the family later on in Italy.

Rome and the Tuscan foothills. She had begged them to stay, entreated, implored them to stay. She would never quarrel, never, never with Julia. There was almost enough money from her little income if they had rolls and cocoa for breakfast and skipped lunch occasionally and the little rooms in Bloomsbury were so very cheap. She had begged Julia to stay, but Julia earned, after years of service, a smug little berth in one of the big metropolitan schools and Josepha helped her with her teaching. Rome and the Tuscan foothills. The drab days, the tired Josepha. And they could stay, they could stay. They could be beggars, anything rather than the dreary treadmill. *Arma virumque cano.* I sing of arms and a god. Was there no god to save his ancient postulates?

It is a very long story or it is a very short story, depending on how you look at it. I could more or less tell it in a paragraph. I could spend my life on ten long volumes and just begin to get the skeleton framework of it. For every life contains the world and sometimes the world is not big enough to contain one life.

But be that extravagant and cryptic statement as it may. Josepha and Midget were torn asunder with all their little untried babyishnesses and all their hypersophistications. The scene of their parting was the railway station at Liverpool. Have you ever been to Liverpool?

Mrs. McAlpin had thrust a little packet into Midget's hand, as is the conventional way of Americans at parting. Midget went hot all over. She had not brought Mrs. McAlpin a present. She had not brought Josepha a present, but she and Josepha had always been too proud to conform to the little courtesies of ordinary human intercourse. She went hot that she had forgotten Julia's present. The length of the station was a tunnel as she stood at the train door. Beyond the tunnel was a substance resembling cotton wool soaked in sulphur. Strips of this substance floated into the station, but even that did not matter, nor even Julia's naggings about being sure to write them and being sure to get a pair of rubbers and being sure to this, to that, to the other thing, because Josepha had disappeared.

The train was to leave in another two minutes. The boat, great and whitewashed in the dingy harbor (they were going second on *Maurisitimania*) was due to leave in another hour or so but the passengers were supposed to be on board at that very moment. This is what always happened when Julia and Josepha were undertaking a long journey. But they never missed a train; they never missed a boat.

However, Midget's train was going. They were waving flags now and the cotton wool was in her throat, the sulphurous cotton wool was clogging her ears, shutting out the sound of shuntings and shoutings and ill-timed bells. Midget, damp and wet, and too long and looped over herself, was succumbing in the corner of the carriage when Josepha fell upon her.

"Here, Wee Witch," she shouted. "I never gave you a present, did I? Didn't I? Here's some chocolates for you. Wee Witches like chocolates—," and she was gone.

My companion said to me, "Surely, it is the best thing."

He had met Josepha in London at one of the studios. She had looked at him brazenly out of her blue eyes. She had said, "He has the manners of an innkeeper's son." She had said that in private to Midget afterwards. She had also added, "I can see with my brain that he is beautiful. I mean that he is beautiful. He is exactly like the Faun. I can realize the shape of his shoulders. I can see the way his head is set. I can see his hands. I am sure he has large feet, solid on the ground, with perfect instep. It is strange how well I can see. They say he has a talent for verse. I know in some way, he is what people say he is. He was very tactful with Mother. Mother adores him. I hate him. I hated him to open the door for you and brush your shoulder. I saw it was delicate. I think him under the surface, unclean."

My companion relit his pipe. He curved his hand about the

pipe bowl and in the early dusk the light shone through the firm, smooth flesh like the sun through the sane, wholesome petals of a garden peony. His arms under his coat were rounded, muscular, yet not overmuscular, not too sinewy, one could see, like the youths who used to pilot the canoeing trips up the Susquehanna River at home.

Across Monte Veccio, the wind blew from the sea. It broke the last brown petals from the late cherry that cut across Vesuvius, from the angle of the Hotel Paradiso balcony, like a tree in a Fuji print. The light lay purple in deeper purple bars above the space the sun had just that second left, a vacuum that drew to it a swirl of changing flecks, flecks changing from gold to deep gold until they slid away or slid together into one even surface of pure metal.

"Finished that Theocritus?"[18]

"Oh, yes," I said.

"Funny," he said, "if these white garlic blossoms should turn out to be leukoion, after all."

"White violets," I said.

"Guess I'll beat it back to my digs," he remarked, then added as an afterthought, "You're not worried about that girl, are you?"

"Oh, Amaryllis in the shade;[19] no, no. I think I managed to probe the construction out with the help of (and thank you) your excellent Liddell and Scott."[20]

"I don't mean Amaryllis," he said from the balcony steps. "I mean the excellent Faustine."[21]

"Faustine?"

"The Transpontine."

"Oh, *Josepha*."

I let myself laugh lightheartedly at his joke. He slid off the balcony steps like a rounded yet perfectly poised and graceful porpoise. He shouted a *buona notte* to the hotel keeper's wife and the little girl, clinging to her skirts in the shadow of the great Capri wine jar. The little girl stepped out from the shadow. The wysteria, rooted in the earthen jar, spilled like ripe wine brushing across her shoulder. She toddled a few steps into the open and waved a perfect little brown Tanagra paw to my companion. She and her mother equally adored the *signor*.

That very afternoon, a group of foreign tourists had intruded on my balcony. It was not my balcony really. It extended the entire length of the hotel. It was really a sort of piazza, very low, only just above the level of the wysteria tops in the three symmetrically placed jars. The group of foreign tourists had gesticulated toward the pear tree, had gesticulated toward the distant wall of Tiberius's ruined villa on the hillside, had gesticulated toward the low walls and the little houses, which only the foam of garden daisies, planted in small wine jars on the roofs, could have proved not immaculately white. They had then returned to the hotel garden and the fronds intruding through the balcony railing and the down-looping tendrils of blossoming osierlike stems, swaying, swaying in the light air from the low roof above their heads, and the bushes, flowering beneath their feet, and the tangle on a level with their nostrils that threatened even the blue wysteria with extinction. They had then taken deep breaths and they had then breathed forth, not unmusically with deep voices, "Ah, tausend Rosen, tausend, tausend Rosen." [22]

Why do I call them foreign tourists? I myself was a foreign tourist, and I have often been told, if there is one thing more objectionable in that line than a German, it is an American.

The thousand roses were beating like the sledgehammer in my brain, against my brain. The thousand, thousand roses. But they could not be because I was sitting inside my little room. I was piling my papers carefully on the table and I was placing the ink pot carefully in the exact middle of the top white sheet so that the night wind should not disarrange them again. I was putting my books straight, exactly straight as an old-maid school mistress arranges her books and papers, arranges and rearranges in fanatic zeal of neatness.

A thousand, thousand roses. The dog that always began barking at the exact moment when day was over and the unholy peace of the southern night began, began barking. Night had come. I wound my watch.

I might read a little; no, the candle was insufficient. I might write a letter. A letter?

To whom should I write a letter? I had no duty letters. My parents were asleep on the other side of the Paridiso garden. To whom should I write? I had no friends I cared for anymore in America.

In America? Where was America? Was there any space or distance? Was there time to be considered as an asset or as a blundering slaves' taskmaster, a slave bound to intimidate, to threaten in his frenzy, blinder slaves? How was there space or distance? A thousand years ago there had been roses, thousand, thousand roses; roses now; roses in the garden where Midget climbed the tree; wysteria there, wysteria here; a pear tree always, always about to blossom, always blossoming.

What had time to say to this? What had space to prove?

A thousand roses, at Paestum once.

Oh you roses, thousand hued, dipped in red wine or sped to death with redder darts of Eros, was that Latin? Who wrote it? Was that translatable?

Oh roses of Paestum,[23] against the rocks of a cruel wall, you broke; nay, it was the wall that broke, its heart rent like the crater of great Aetna because your hand, oh passer by, dipped in a baser heat, touched not to rapture anymore—oh anymore anything. Wall, Moonlight, Peasblossom.[24]

The roses ceased boating against the battered fortress of Midget's brain. She was a girl not altogether without self-control. The young Englishman was not a bad sort, not at all a bad companion for her. She dipped her forehead in the earthenware basin, dabbed cold water at the base of her neck. She did her hair in two tight, unbecoming rat tails.

There seemed thunder in the air. She fastened the French windows opening onto the balcony. It was very dark.

Her companion had said, "Surely, it's the best thing." He had spoken callously. He hated Josepha.

Midget repeated it coldly. Her feet, she noticed, were marked with the rim of her shoes where the rim of her shoes let in the dust. Yet her feet looked very white on the dark red tiling of the floor. Her feet were very cold but she could not get into bed. The dog was howling but he always howled.

The hounds of Hecate might have dogged Josepha's footprints. Perhaps it was just as well. She had written, "I am going to marry—I will be married when you get this—a passable person. He gives University Extension lectures.[25] We may get across to Berlin in the spring." She gave no details, no explanation for her sudden *volte-face*. (She had always repudiated all talk or thought of marriage.)

She added as a postscript, "Perhaps some day Wee Witches will grow up."

FOUR

Vulgar Details

T HE fiancé was beating the end of his stick frantically against the opposite side of the taxicab, making the little vase, which mercifully held no artificial flowers, jump violently as if to emphasize his already overemphasized assertions.

"Can't you see," he shouted above the buzz and roar of the Piccadilly traffic and above the little personal buzz and roar of their own slightly disjointed taxi wheels, "Can't you see what she's up to? Can't you ever see anything?"

Midget sat very stiff in the corner. She wore her hat, a thing she never used to do in a taxicab. She answered very seriously, "No, Raymond, I can't."

He suddenly stopped jabbing with his stick. He jerked toward her. "Can't what," he said, forgetting his fury of assertiveness.

"Can't what you said," answered Midget," "can't ever see anything."

The erstwhile fiancé flung his hat on the taxi floor. "Damn," he said.

They were speeding from Victoria, from the hotel where Josepha (on the way to Berlin) was staying with her husband, into the backwater of Bloomsbury, to the little lodging house where Josepha had once stayed with Midget.

"You can't go on this way," said Raymond. "I, as your nearest male relative, protest."

"That is why I thought I might run away with them to Dresden," said Midget.

Midget, seated precariously on the edge of the bed, upstairs in her little room, reviewed it all. She still wore her hat. One gloved hand rested on the white rail at the foot of the bed. She looked like a young lady on a boat near Geneva, with head bent forward, poetically and pensively regarding the limpid water. She looked young and sentimental and smug, you might have said. It was the gray glove dangling in the other hand that gave you that impression.

She caught sight of herself in the spotted glass of the wardrobe opposite. "I am glad I am not what I look like," she said. She heard herself say it. Then she spoke a few more words to the blue image in the spotted mirror.

I am not going to repeat to you the words. She seemed to be arguing with herself quite clearly about something the Raymond person had jabbed into her consciousness. She seemed to consider what the Raymond had said, not so much in the light of criticism of the people of whom he had spoken, as of a comment on Raymond himself. "Do other people think things like that," she said. "And I thought I had got over being surprised at Raymond."

Raymond had put the matter bluntly. So crudely that it seemed impossible that such things could have any possible bearing upon life. Raymond had said, "I thought you had more sense. As for J, you know what I have always thought of her. She told me herself in the Botanical Gardens" (so, they had found time in all the rush and crush that very afternoon, for the Botanical Gardens) "that she had married him on a strict understanding—er —oh well, that they were to travel a little, and then if—er—it could be proved—well, they could be divorced the following year."

"If what could be proved?" asked Midget.

"That," stammered the erstwhile in a frenzy of inspiration, "there had been no children."

"I see," said Midget. "And if there had been children?" Did the erstwhile think her, in the way American men have of thinking nice American women, a fit inmate for an asylum for incurable cretins?

Raymond ignored her question. He continued, "You see, she doesn't even care for him."

"You could hardly make such an arrangement with a person you did care for," replied Midget to his apparently irrefutable statement.

"Don't you see," reposted the Raymond, with a little upward quiver of triumph in his voice, "*that* is the reason you must not go with them."

"I don't see," said Midget. "She says she needs me. *He* says she will be lonely as he must be away all day and she has already heard all his lectures. I think it very tactful. He didn't even suggest my coming to the lectures."

"This is the reason you must not go," he went on, talking as if she had not answered him at all. "She is in love with that Irish dramatist that crossed with them on the boat." [26] (Midget, determined not to be surprised at anything, sat a little—but not to Raymond's eyes appreciably—stiffer in the taxi corner.) "The dramatist, she told me, had arranged the marriage. The fortunate husband is a friend of his. They are to meet abroad later in the summer. Josepha thinks she is clever. I myself have played my little game of chess in my own time. You are the *bon bouche*. She told me already Seaford is your victim. *Partie carrée*. All very pretty, all very chaperoned, Madame, you see, and her friend, and madame's husband, and the other person, well, I suppose they will call him the brother of the friend of Madame."

"Rot," said Midget. There was absolutely no limit whatever to the lengths Raymond's imagination could take, once loosed. She had not known Raymond so long nor been engaged to Raymond so long ago for nothing.

The taxi had stopped with a jerk. They had apparently arrived. Raymond, fumbling in the gloom, paid the driver and tipped, as Raymond always did, too much. Midget asked him to sit on the steps and talk it over. He jumped as if he thought she really meant it and shriveled against a lamppost. "Goodnight," said Midget.

"Do wait," shivered Raymond's voice from the darkness. If he had only known, it was more compromising to stand dragging out this hectic, pleading conversation by the lamppost than secluded in the hall beyond the unheeding doors.

Midget waited on the lowest step.

"The fortunate husband is not badly off. I have seen worse assorted pairs." Raymond's voice had steadied itself, whether at triumph for this parting thrust, whether with superb consciousness of himself, proven man of the world, himself with his little game of chess in his own time, or whether with a memory of a Midget and wild violets and a sort of madness he had used to check, a madness not altogether assumed but used by her to taunt him with on mad occasions when the wind was high or the first frost of winter flower or bell berries had opened in the brown leaves. Raymond's voice was quiet. "You know yourself what her life is. You know no damn woman stands a chance when you're around. You might leave them alone together, at least till they've fixed it up one way or the other about the separation."

My companion said, "Raymond was right then." He might have said, but somehow his delicacy did not permit such an outspoken statement: "*I* was right then." However, he was English and of another world and it was much pleasanter reviewing the irreparable past with him than with Raymond, who always interrupted with a "Dear child, I tried to make you read so, so, so and so" (that one had just radiantly discovered on ones own) "ten years ago," or "*How* many years have I been trying to teach you to wash your face?"

The light filtered through the yellow gauze Liberty curtain onto the polished surface of the dark walnut table. Outside, Piccadilly traffic hummed and sang. It sang as the traffic of no city in the world, a deep drowning, a completely transmuting, a revealing and a restraining sound. All those words are exactly what I mean. Have you heard New York shriek real terror, real emotion, reality, Europe and Asia in one voice, swift, penetrating, intimate and unrepentant? Have you heard Paris at night? London at teatime when one is sheltered from the crowd, gives one, as no city in the world gives one, a background.

My companicn and I had strolled into the tea shop early. We found a table by the widow. His black velvet elbow kept the yellow gauze curtain from unbalancing the slight stems of the blue hyacinths placed upright in the shallow bowl. I had heard him say, "Raymond was right then," but that had been some time ago, before the tea arrived, and so I answered with, "Do they really grow wild in England?"

I had met a number of hangers-on of studios in America and a few more select specimens in Paris and in London, but I had never met anyone in my life before who understood the other half or the explanatory quarter of the part of the sentences I left unsaid. Not that it took great clairvoyance to realize what I meant, but a very little clairvoyance means a very great deal in a world where there is almost none.

"Pools of them," he said, "in the woods and small rivers washing the edges of the fields." When he finished deciding whether to take another cress sandwich or a salmon one, I asked him, pretending I had forgotten the first thing he had said, if he had seen Raymond lately.

He said yes. "*Did* you know he was engaged?"

If my companion had been an American youth, I should have

inevitably answered, "What again?" As it was, out of respect to his own delicacy and out of loyalty to the ancient Raymond, I answered with a slightly amazed, half-interrogatory inflection, "Oh?"

It seemed to have been an English lady this time. We were all to meet her, though it was very select, at someone or other's mutual friend's studio tea.

"Leukothea,"[27] said my companion, when I had finished pouring out his second cup of tea. "I think these Anglo-American marriages are the very best, don't you?"

I had already told him what I thought.

"What exactly *did* Josepha write Raymond, Basil?" I said.

Josepha had written Midget exactly nothing at all. She had written at regular intervals, during the month since her departure, reams to Raymond. She had written in her stilted, perfected style her stilted, perfected and sometimes startlingly penetrating views on the personalities she had met, on the reception she and her husband had been accorded at the various university centers through which they had passed on their lecture tour. Raymond had more or less hurled those letters at Midget in a bunch. Then they stopped coming. "Why," asked Midget, "doesn't she write any more?" "I suppose," Raymond had replied, "because I've never answered one of the damn things."

The horse chestnuts were burning ardent white and laurel-pink and again white and white flambeaus throughout the parks. Spring that year seemed of an interminable and flaunting beauty. It had begun in Italy, when Josepha had written as of a long-distant time. "We might get across to Berlin in the spring." It had followed Midget, like the hours the robes of Venus, up to the Tuscan foothills. The pale almonds that had died in Rome almost before December met her, like the face of a lost lover in the valleys of the Loire. Again wisteria that had died and come again to birth against the yellow palace walls of Venice, here in London, tangled its memories in her heart, like the oak trees in the flaming locks of Absolum, and did her heart to death. What had time to say to this? What could space prove?

Yet time was threatening her now. Time who had cheated her of time, seemed to jibber at her, to demand repayment for the hours lost in dreaming. You would cheat time, it said, see now, how time cheats you. You put off the day of reckoning, it said, see how the day draws near. Horse chestnuts were flaring ardent rose across the parks. And this was June.

"It's no use, Margaret," said Mrs. Defreddie. "You must go back with us."

The window of their little flat in Chelsea was open toward the city square of verdure. From afar came a steady underhum of traffic. "I can't go back," said Midget.

Her mother, with the pretty eyes and the high Flemish forehead, dropped her bit of fine embroidery and regarded Midget. The pretty eyes looked puzzled. Perhaps in all her life (except in the way of new fears of new sorts of measles or worries about the comparative merits of Miss Morton or the Chesterton School or whether the Leighton dancing class was, after all, the best thing but then, of course, her brothers always took her), Midget had never caused the pretty eyes annoyance. At least, she had never willfully done so. She had never in all her life, as far as, now standing by the window, she could in any way recall it, said to her mother, "I can't," or to her father, "I won't."

It is true at the time of the early Raymond episode, she had broken from them. That had caused pain, but it was a subterranean sort of struggle. It was a question of atmosphere and pressure and tyranny of affections, but Midget had never faced a direct issue with absolute defiance.

Standing now a the window of the little flat in Chelsea, with the underhum of traffic in her ears, she knew that Time had her by the throat.

Time had her by the throat, yet there were still several ways, at least in part, to circumvent him. He obviously was Victor, yet the victim knew, as a young marquise may know, though the guillotine await her at the top of a very short yet interminably long flight of steps, that many things may happen between the last footfall on the topmost step and the ten spaces or so that are still left her to be trodden in the sunlight. Many, many things may happen, things very insignificant, perhaps, to us casual beholders, but to her of uttermost importance. She might, for instance, poor little lady, tread upon her skirt hem. What calamity. She might, after her valiant ascent of the small flight of interminable yet finally terminated steps, fall, in a faint, face downward in the sunlight. Ah, but no. A marquise may faint becomingly in a ballroom, never on the road to her destruction! What then might happen? A rose pressed in the little feverish palm to comfort her, from the tapering and doomed fingers of some companion of the past, about to follow her in her calamity? Many things might happen, but one all-sustaining hope was left to outdazzle petty thoughts of final comfort: a head held high, a pace, unhurried yet unfaltering, a little marquise victorious over victory, and her doom.

Time had her by the throat. Midget thought, as the proverbial drowning man, of many little things she had till now forgotten. It was that curious flash into the past that made her tremble for her conquest of the Victor. The present was easy enough. She had, for the last few feverish nights, rehearsed her little speech. "I should have rebelled long ago. It is not that I am callous. I have really, and that has been the trouble from the first, been far too tender-hearted. I have not been half rebellious enough. If I had begun at fifteen instead of now, things would have been all right. I should never, never have submitted to geometry. I always hated all the girls you chose for me as friends. I am exactly ten years behind in my development, because I should have gone away from home when I was fifteen, into a shop; hats, dressmakers, assistant, anything, anything—" and in the night, in her thoughts, her voice rose clearer, sharper, more intense and crushing as the anythings crowded faster and faster, with more and more fury, upon each other's heels—"anything, I should have known, rather than stay at home."

This was one speech. It varied slightly in manner but the matter was the same whether the speech came, cold and sedate, before breakfast, just as her mother was beginning to flutter with the hope of American mail, or whether it were casually spoken of while waiting for a bus or in a taxi, seeing the sights of Hampton Court, or on the bench, watching the pigeons outside the British Museum. The pigeons, for instance, would prove an excellent beginning: "Oh, mother, that purple pigeon would look lovely on a hat." Hat. That was the clue. Dressmaking, milliners, girls earning their own living. Must begin early. "I should have gone away from home when I was fifteen etc. etc., etc." The excellent mother appealed to on the practical side and on the side of abstract wisdom, and the deed was done.

There was another speech. That speech she could not rehearse in words. That speech was a hot wave across her brain. A fear possessed her, a fear that if they did not let her go, something terrible and tragic would eat out her heart and close over her head and beat her back, back into the present, when her feet were shod with fire as with wings and her spirit was dragging them, those fire-shod feet, far and high into the future, into the past that tread with purple robes and into the future, white lover of the past. There were no words to this speech. A fear possessed her that suddenly she might find words to this speech, that she might shout or sing those words, and that they would break, those good and simple people, shriveled to ash, before her utterance, or that they might seize her, somehow tear the firy sandals from her feet and bind her down forever.

"But why don't you want to go back?" said Mrs. Defreddie. "Don't your remember we only just had your bedroom repapered before you left?"

Midget turned with a little jerk. Her face, if her mother had but seen it, was white with passion and a strange light filled the eyes whose gray iris was drowned out in blackness.

Midget began her speech. The words were quite different from those she had rehearsed or those she had anticipated. "You know," she almost stuttered in her frenzy to be done with it. "I didn't stay with the Westons as I said I was going to while father was ill. I didn't even tell you, when I wrote to Bournemouth. I was alone in the little place in Bloomsbury where I had been with the McAlpins."

It was the first heart-burning confession she had ever made, of what might almost have been called her first deception.

Her mother seemed scarcely to have comprehended. Perhaps she had not even heard her. Mrs. Defreddie said, "What a very good thing Josepha is married." Her tone seemed to imply, "What a very lucky thing she ever got a husband, and so very unexpected."

Midget saw, as the proverbial drowning man, many things she thought she had forgotten. It was that curious flash into the past that had unnerved her. She trembled for her conquest of the Victor.

She had forgotten even Josepha. How did Orestes [28] feel when he held the knife to slay his mother? What did Orestes see? What did Orestes think?

Long, level plains of Sparta, set close against the foothills, were they so very different from the garden that spread through the Pennsylvania valleys? Was the river into which Orestes slipped his little painted boats so very different from their river? Was his mother, set with her massive bracelets, whose gracious head bent down to kiss his fingers where he slashed them with his jeweled handled javelin, gift of a king to a king's son (when he cut those very painted boats from fragrant poplar), so very different from any other woman bending to comfort any other child of any other king?

What did Orestes feel? Something unnerved him. Not the present. Things, as the present draw them, were dire and evil and to be combatted. What of the past?

"Your mother has betrayed your father," spoke the present to

Orestes. "Your mother, your mother, your mother," the present said to Midget, "has betrayed, or would betray, through the clutch and the tyranny of the emotion, your father, the mind in you, the jewel the king, your father gave you as your birthright. Look," said the present, "and choose. Here is a knife, slay your mother. She has betrayed or would betray that gift."

The mind of Midget looked and the soul of Midget held the weapon, steel white, her frozen heritage. The soul of Midget spoke words unrehearsed and unexpected to the mind of Midget. "Do you remember those marzipan fruits she used to get you? She redressed that hopeless doll many, many times when any other mother would have flung it on the dust heap. What of that birthday when she put morning glories through the string of every birthday parcel and addressed each of the eight separate parcels with a separate pet name? What of that wonderful convalescence from scarlet fever when you found on your pillow—"

"Stop," said the mind of Midget.

Knowing that she was defeated, she turned to rend the object of her downfall. The object, ignorant of the storm she was occasioning, said, "Margaret dear, do you think Gladys would prefer blue or pink forget-me-nots for Sissie's bonnet?" She held up Sissie's bonnet at this moment, for Margaret's inspection.

It was then that Margaret stamped. It was then that Midget exploded.

"Do I care for Sissie," she shouted. "Do I care for Gladys? How many times must I tell you, Mother, that I hate them all. How many thousand times must I repeat that I am not coming back. You are tyrannizing me. You are hurting me. It hurts me to see you sit there, so placid, not knowing, not caring about other people's lives. Not really caring. Not really knowing. You don't know. You never cared for Josepha. Do you think it was a surprise to me that Josepha married? Everyone adored her. There were a dozen men in London who were mad about Josepha—"

"But I thought you were so *fond* of Sissie," said her mother. Midget sat on the floor and cried.

She sobbed it out, not what she had rehearsed, not what she had expected. She seemed to be sobbing a confession when all the time, above her head, her mind stood, just above her head, and in its hands, a steel white javelin.

She saw herself on the floor. She might have been fifteen and all the ten years, her years, yet to live. All the ten years her mind was clamoring for, all the ten years the mind with white-pointed javelin was waiting to avenge.

She was defeated. She was not Orestes. She was a girl. Yet she was not Electra, the sister, who waited,[29] though her heart was breaking to help Orestes. She was not Electra. She was not Orestes. Had she been one or the other, she would have won.

"Of course, I cared. Of course, I cared. I cared from the first. But I couldn't tell you. How could I tell you? After all the mess we all made of everything when I thought I'd marry Raymond. You don't suppose I'd have let him follow us about like that if I hadn't cared awfully. No, I'm not engaged. After the Raymond fiasco, I couldn't be engaged. I won't be engaged. But I'm going to marry Basil. No, no, no. Just marry him. No one is to come. *No* one. We are going to a registrar's or whatever it is's office. *No* one is to come."

The little maid came with the tea things and Midget went to wash her face.

FIVE

Snow and Ash

THERE was a war.[30] A cloud. Five years. Already a few months before the actual panic, old Professor Defreddie and Midget's mother had returned to America. Midget had married Basil, as she threatened, quietly in a registrar's office. All that was long and long ago. Time had them by the throat. Time had the world by the throat, shaking and shaking, evil and vicious. Shaking the world till its head was numb and its heart wrenched from its body. Shaking and shaking and never letting it go. Until the world seemed mercifully past its agony, about to perish, and there was peace.

A cloud. Five years.

Before that cloud, that past trailed robes of purple, beyond the cloud, the future stood, avid, radiant, white lover of the past. A cloud. Five years. This was the present. A flame about a city. Small city railings splintered and city parks infested with a black trail of livid, wretched creatures who shivered against each other as the crash came nearer. Who woke as from a dream when distant rumblings died away, and scurried like black rats, fleeing the sinking wreck, washing up on the pavements, as if from the city about to sink, fleeing, black lines to subterranean safety.

Who was there in the world that mattered? What mattered? The present was dead. They were all dead. As a little marquise while waiting in prison lifts the ring against her cheek, to hear the magic tune, sounding beneath the flat enamel setting, reminder of the exotic, curious past, so Midget sometimes, turning a sudden corner in the darkness, cried to her wretched heart her *cras amet*.

> *Cras amet qui nunquam amavit*
> *quique amavit cras amet.*

Tomorrow let him love, for today is dead. All about her, people cried of nobility, of sacrifice; all the world was led to its devotion to sacred duty. All the world was splendid and heroic. Every soul she knew. All had some song of duty or distinction. Someone they knew, someone had proved high servant, archpriest or sacred offering to duty. What was her duty?

> *Cras amet qui nunquam amavit.*

Let him love tomorrow who has never loved. Who never has loved. That meant everyone, almost everyone. There was no love, save love of duty, love of sacrifice. Love tomorrow for there is no love today.

After all, when all is said and done, then sentiment is stowed away with other relics of the pleasant half dream, the pleasant half waking that London had allowed her for a few months before the terror fell, after all, when loyalty and sentiment were stowed away, who was this person that came back to her, with the smell of gas in his breath, with the stench of death in his clothes? "How the war has improved Basil," she heard on all sides. True, there had been plenty of room for improvement in Basil as there always is in any of us. But was this improvement?

She dragged out the old books. She dragged out the old

threadbare Latin tags they had flung to one another, so ingen-
uously, beneath the olives that wisted from the peaks of Monte
Veccio and crept and fell and bent and clung and tangled themselves up with themselves and the rocks and the stone walls and
drew back to leave space for a little field of blue flax or a tiny
rocky vineyard and then fell, one last sheer daring feat of splendid grace into the sea itself. The tags that to her now seemed all
of life worth keeping left Basil with a faraway stare, perfectly
listless, perfectly indifferent. He was seeing perhaps heroicly
into the present, into the present that was dead. Into death,
itself. He was, she found even in the earliest days, a part of it
all. He was taking his stand with it. You might, not inoppor-
tunely, ask, how could he do otherwise? And Midget would have
answered, and would answer still. "You can go and fight, and get
dragged into the mire of falsity and murder and yet know it false.
You can die with a lie on your lips and yet know it false. You can
kill your own fellow officer as he sleeps beside you or you can
kill the enemy climbing the ridge with rhymes of a vast mountain, sweet upon his lips, and know still that both are false.
Knowing all, all is false, you can yet stay true to the one star,
yourself, your very self, you can do all this and still retain your
self, your soul; your own, unswerving."

Midget felt that Basil was not playing true to himself, that was
all. He did not believe in the comradeship he spoke of. He did
not believe in the dastardly enemy he spoke of. If he had believed, Midget would not have minded. At least, it would have
been his star. Even if it were not hers, she could have accepted
his standards for himself, if he had accepted them himself.

There was a church in Laodicea we have all heard about from
our earliest infancy. Basil was that church.

So it was, when she had lost her companion,[31] and the world
was fretting about her and the world was yapping at her ankles
when she dared move, as if to make some tentative slight friendship with one of its inmates, as Cerberus might have yapped at

Psyche sent on her mission into Hell,[32] so it was that Midget found a new trick of seeing.

The trick was not altogether a good trick. I have my reasons for saying this. It shut her out from life. You might argue that life had or was trying to shut her out from it. But life is not a thing you can argue about. A cloud. Five years. It came. It lifted. You cannot argue about a tidal wave. You escape it if you can.

A tidal wave does one of two things. Either it swirls you into it, with a million others of your sort, and swirls you about (if it be more or less a metaphorical tidal wave as this one is) and you, all being together in the same swirl, are all in a way comfortably heroic and out of the dead run of the common level of usual sea. Or else it slashes you out, in the crest, as it were, high, high above the rest of itself and the rest of humanity. This is a very marvelous sensation to the few thus chosen to be the high froth or the high nothingness of the wave itself.

It is a pleasant sensation to behold the great mass, and the flow and black lift of it, beneath you. It is not an altogether healthy nor wholesome nor sane feeling to feel as Midget did, so thoroughly out of touch with all humanity. It is true, she was more or less used to feeling out of things. But that was in America, where the feeling as I have described it was more concentrated, more rotund. She and Josepha, those orient pearls, were yet a decorative unit; or at least were materialized, so to speak; from the oyster's point of view, truly a blemish, but to the connoisseur and beauty lover, not altogether without value.

The trick was not altogether a good trick. Brindel, whom we are going to hear of later, said to Midget, "When I first saw you, you were like a volcano, blazing and roaring beneath, but all the surface covered with snow and ash."

Snow and ash, you might have said this trick was. Not the pearl reflecting all minute and vivid landscapes, tiny, tiny surfaces, color of purple bean flower or faint tint of thistle. Not the pearl; sanity, life, salvation. It was not a good trick of dreaming. But what can you ask of life hurling the very heart and passion and beauty of itself high, high above, to perish as it will or drift to far distances, transformed to rain or subtler weight of other?

Josepha wrote after many years of silence.

A drowning man may clasp a slab of marble to his heart, knowing too well that it will only hasten his sinking.

Midget's first impulse, seeing the familiar script, was to scratch across it with a firm, defiant pen, "Not known." But already American Express had scratched out the first address in forwarding the letter and there was scarcely any space for fresh inditings. Then, too, the stamp proved treacherous to Midget's better, sterner impulse. So Josepha and her husband were still in Italy!

Midget turned over the envelope and saw the return address (as if Josepha were not sure if it would reach her) Fiesole, Firenze, Italia. It was like Josepha to put Firenze, Italia.

Italia. Thou hast the fatal gift of beauty.[33]

The fatal gift, as might have been expected, proved too much for Midget.

She smelled the envelope first, suspecting a stray hint of orange or of the citron blossoms that surround Mirandola's villa on the hillside. There was no scent of flowers but there was a warmth somehow, somewhere about the letter. Midget was not a clairvoyant, but she knew by the feel of this that Josepha was in some strange state of peril.

She held the envelope to the light. She could decipher no word through the firm yet light crackle of foreign paper. She shook the envelope. The sheets—she judged a number of them —were packed tight, allowing no space for wandering. Was the letter, after all, not some cold stab at her affection but another tribute?

A drowning man may clasp a slab of marble to his heart. But

perhaps after all this weight within her hands was an altar, or an altar step leading to an altar, dedicated to some fatal gift of beauty.

Some fatal gift of beauty.

Do you think I ever look at those white iris buds in the garden without thinking? There are some mimosa blossoms dropping on my paper now while I write. Do you remember that night we spent in Liverpool before the boat left? You always were a fool. I didn't really see those ghost pigeons on the window ledge. You thought I saw them. How could they possibly have been there? Why did you always believe in all the lies I told you? Do you know why? Because you never grew up. Even in America, I told you lies. I told them worse in Europe because you can lie to yourself better here. You can make yourself think you see things better here. I never saw any of the things I pretended to see. Once when I was very ill, or was pretending to be very ill, because it made Mama and Grandmama run about more and fuss more, I really did see a lot of blue sparrows or bluebirds fly and fly and fly around, above the bed. I watched and watched and watched until I was dizzy. Then I tried to faint and, joy, Mother rushed and Grandmama rushed and I was IT. I always wanted to be IT. That was such a success, those birds, that I went on trying different stunts. There was a cat. There was a large dog and several people and a horrible creature, a beggar; I kept her for particular occasions, said she was trying to steal me —la, la—Mama's little pet complex. I caught her many times. How did I know all about *those* awful facts without ever, ever being told? I'll tell you how. I have come to the conclusion that Mama never married my father. At least, I suppose I hope it so much that it almost seems true. But why did she never show me his picture or tell me anything? She always said, "Darling, I lived with him two years in the forest. He promised there would be no baby. When there was I ran away and stayed with your grandmama. I wanted a boy. You weren't exactly what I asked for!" Then she would cry and be loving and I would promise to go with her to communion next Sunday. I myself don't think she ever married him. Is that why I pretend to see things I don't see? *You* might tell me. You are the only wise person I ever knew and I liked you because I could tell you the most lies.

I suppose you have had marvelous and angelic séances with the Basil-pot. I mean the pot of Basil.[34] Does he apotheosize your beauty in his immortal verse? I do hope he gets killed in the war. But, dear flutter heart, cease fluttering. He won't. That fat, sleek, beautiful youth type never do.

What do you think? The peasants keep asking me if I will bear the Christo. Of course, I tell them, si, si, si, si. Suppose I did. That would be a joke. He will be a Christo or a bore. I think he may be a bore. I shall send him then to school. Of course, it will be a him. You will have a her. You will have a sort of witch thing that will know all that you don't know.

Seaford sends his love. He still thinks that you think he was trying to tamper with your virtue when you refused to come with us to Dresden. Why did you refuse, little fool? To stay and marry Basil-pot. Of course I almost forgot the pot.

I said, didn't I, that the white iris had a bud or two? But now in one minute they have opened. Do you know why, little fool? Because I can hardly write, and this is the first time I have not lied to you. Because if I scream they will all come running out, and for once they bore me with their fussings. I am not going to scream.

"The doctor is a Sienese—at least he used to live there. He thought oxygen was advisable and the tins are standing, waiting to resuscitate one or both. Both. Me and a piece of me like that slimy Seaweed that propagates itself by breaking off itself. It ought to be born by night.

Josepha.

Midget wrote:

Josepha:

Were they lies? I wonder if they were lies. When I used not to see things in America, I believed always in what you saw. Now that I see things for myself, I wonder if you really do see things. I wonder if you really do see things because I wonder (after I have seen them) if I really do see things myself.

Josepha. I have not forgotten you. I pretend that I have forgotten you because I pretend that I have forgotten everything. I have a new game. I am a shell. There is nothing in the shell.

You used to tell me all sorts of things like this. You used to say, "Your *eyes* seem to see, why don't *you* see?"

I will tell you why I never saw, except that once or twice when we knew that we were other people. I had too much to eat and too many people about me. It is wrong, it is a vice not to eat enough. But how can you help it when the bread is full of cinders and a little lump of bacon takes all afternoon waiting in a line, and then maybe you don't get it. You saw things often because you and Julie were such self-conscious fools (I am using your own overworked little word) about your poverty.

Julia was really rather pleased to be indigent. It was a sort of substitution for happiness. She was happy in being unhappy. So were you. But it lifted you and Julia out of the great mass of the mediocrities I dwelled among who hated unhappiness and suspected poverty.

Now I am poor. Now I am rich.

I have a lover—not Basil.

I don't see him very often, but I know he is there. He is a distinguished poet.

I suppose you might say I was a spiritual prostitute, but I don't think so; no, I don't think so, because I have only one lover and he is a great poet.

You might say that he is one of those evil things you read about in great tomes, who come and seduce women, those ghouls or whatever. You know what I mean, from Anatole France we read on the boat crossing. But he is not a ghoul. He is a spirit. He is a great poet.

We don't know each other very well yet. We simply meet by accident in the woods, or in the little house in the woods. We usually look and look at one another. Sometimes he says a poem. Sometimes it grows dark and my ecstasy becomes so great that I leave him there alone and come back myself to my room and try to read and try to work. Sometimes I write a poem. Of course, none as beautiful as his poems.

In the house we have in the woods, you could be as well as not. It is a Roman house. It is very small, low, with columns, the ice white stones stand sheer on the floor of the forest. There ought, I suppose to be a square of grass about the place, but the moss and Virginia creeper and poison ivy and little toadstools shove right up against the stones of the floor. They do not break through the floor like the English stonecrop in the old gardens here. It is as if the stones froze them back.

I have hardly looked inside the house, except for the first little entrance hall which is rather dark and has a whortleberry crimson blanket on the floor. If my lover asks me to come into the room beyond, I run away at once. I do not think I am afraid or shy. It simply does not seem fitting, or it does not seem the time to see him or something. I almost prefer finding the place empty because then I sit in the sunlight in the porch and lean my head against a pillar and sleep. That is queer, isn't it? To sleep in one's sleep.

You might think the light was very shallow in this forest. Shallow—that is quite an idea. The word shallow came of itself just as my lover slides of himself, without being called, without being expected, around a pillar or out of the door when I am just going to sleep on the whortleberry-colored blanket. You might think the light was shallow in this forest. You would think, I think, that it would be a sort of a silver, a glorified gray. I would think so if I used my imagination. But the light is very full and rich. The light is very warm. The light has a whole, crumbling feeling about it, you know, like when you crumble out the center of a dogwood blossom and the pollen dusts your fingers. The light seems to dust your fingers but it does not really.

I will not tell you exactly what my lover looks like nor what he wears for you would laugh and say you thought it very like a cheap steel engraving of an idealized eighteenth-century portrait of Catullus.[35] My description would give that idea. But if you say, Catullus, Catullus, Catullus often enough like a charm (though I don't think my lover is Catullus), you will get some idea of the color of the things he wears.

This color does not match nor does it clash with the whortleberry blanket.

Myself, though I never went barefoot much and am afraid of my feet, have on no shoes and neither am afraid of my feet nor care about them one way or another. I know that they are brown like my hands and arms. My hair is not done up in any particular way, pushed anyhow into a band. I am not in keeping with the columns of the porch.

I think it is my body that lives there and my soul here. I am more soulful-looking here than there.

Here I look at myself too much in the glass. Sometimes I say to it, "There is *one* person I recognize." Perhaps I look as odd to other people as other people look to me. Well, of course, I know I must. Though the little boys here never shout at one as they do in America.

When my lover wrote, "Thy hyacinth hair, thy classic face," he was thinking of you when, that day, the morning and evening star sang. When he wrote, "Ah, psyche, from the regions which,"[36] he was thinking of me when I stand with my clothes off and admire myself, turned half sideways in the glass.

Did my soul get transmuted here by some chance and does my body wait for it there with my lover? Will they come together some day, my soul and my body?

I know that this is not about Basil and your baby and saying polite things about Seaford and explaining about the reason I never came to Dresden.

Do you remember the very first hyacinths[37] were out that day your train left? Your arms were full of them and your eyes hated me above them and you seemed to say, "You see there are other people, you see there are other hyacinths than the ones you bring me."

Yes, you tell lies, Josepha. There were never other hyacinths.

Midget.

Midget wrote:

Josepha:

Some day Wee Witches will grow up. You wrote to me at Capri, "Some day Wee Witches will grow up." Did you mean this? Is this to be grown up to see a face over your bed at night?

But I did not see it often. I really saw it only once. There are so many different ways of thinking you see things. You can imagine. That is one process. You can go to sleep and dream an ordinary dream. That is another way. An ordinary dream is like ordinary thoughts, things you think and don't care about, things not bad enough to make you conscious of their badness nor clear enough to make you happy. Imagination is different. There are dreams that are like imagination. There is another kind of dream that is not imagination nor ordinary dream. Often you forget it. Sometimes you remember the feeling of it and not it, itself.

That dream is to ordinary dream what this face I saw is to ordinary imagination.

The face was my lover's face. Do you know those white, water-lily magnolias? I suppose I thought the words he said. He said, "Helen thy beauty."[38]

Is poetry enchantment? Have people forgotten what poetry is? You used to know what poetry is? Do you remember how you made me say "Swallow" to you? Do you remember "Thy way is long to the sun and the south"? Do you remember "the wild birds take flight and follow and find the sun"?[39]

Were those the wild birds you saw, the blue bluebirds or, as you said, blue sparrows? Wasn't it sparrows that drew the chariot of the goddess?

Do you think the goddess might be the mother of you and my lover and of me? Could she be our mother, not a flaming sword?

My lover looks wistful enough. I don't believe "Helen thy beauty" eased his heart. Nothing will ease your heart. Nothing will ease mine.

You think your baby is going to make you happy. Perhaps he will. Perhaps you will fear him and hate him and never confess your fear or your hate to anyone or to yourself. Perhaps your mother hated you. Perhaps my mother hated me. Perhaps the mother of my lover hated him and that has made us waifs and fugitive.

Is it hatred that has made us poets, or love?

Why did you never learn Latin? You say you speak Italian. I never could say more than a word or so to the drivers and the waiters. Basil spoke fluently to everyone.

You will never know what that line feels like that finishes "*cede virgo Delia.*"[40]

Has the maid of Delos departed from you now that you have your baby?

I feel something has departed from the world now that you have your baby. I don't know what has departed. Things look black now everywhere. I look into blackness when I close my eyes. There was beauty inside before I had your letter. Now the beauty inside is one with the black without.

Perhaps I pray the maid of Delos to bend over you. For she knew the world of blackness. She was Hecate in hell.

Hecate was a Wee Witch grown up.

Will I ever find my mother? Let him love today who never

has loved. Do love's feet burn in Hell till even the embers grow ash before him and the flames dwindle to sea-wafted mist?

The maid of Delos treaded upon the sand. She caught the weed and shells that clung to the amber weed stems. She twisted and flung them like a serpent's scourge, like the Medusa's hair. She frightened us and then she laughed and then she ran in pity, until we believed she was our mother with the violets in her hair.

Her face was like our mother's face. She was sister to our mother. She culled us close to her, more loving than a mother, because her arms were hungry. Nothing would ease her heart.

Almost we loved her more than our lost mother because her heart was always unappeased. Almost we would give her anything to make her smile.

Why did she run to snatch the rabbit from the night owl, why did she keep the sparrow from the hawk?

Why did she loosen the hawk upon the young kid? Why did she fill the hearts of men with envy?

Oh maid of Delos, tread upon the seacoast. Spread whitened sand beneath the feet of strangers, because our friends are faithless.

See, oh Josepha, great in your pride, I have made a bitter prayer at last. To spite you and to spite myself and to spite your glorious baby.

Sleep, Josepha. Are you dead? What is this birth you speak of? I would cry if I had any tears. Sleep, Josepha. Are you dead?

If you are dead, I will make a song for you, because my lover and myself are friendless.

Midget.

SIX

Sister of Charmides

BASIL had written, sending a photograph of an old French chateau, saying that he was happier than he had been for years, sent back from the lines, because of some slight recurrence of the trouble caused by that first year's gas attack. There were wild boars in the forest, and little deer. Basil wrote as he had not written since those days in Italy. It was because the letter brought back the memory of broken vineyard walls and sprays of wild gladiolas—red almost to black—against them, and the small rose and purple pulse (he always knew the quaint separate English country names for them) pushing so strong and coarse, for all their delicacy between the uneven stones that pretended to make a pathway among the scattered olives, that something in the jesting half-banter of the letter hurt.

There was no harm in his calling her sister of Charmides.[41] It was, in its casual way, just like the thoughtful, flattering young Englishman who had befriended her against the Americans in Rome. "I came to Rome to see Rome and devils and ghosts and the yellow Tiber," she had raged at her poor mother, almost in hysteria, one day, "not just the very same kind of people we used to have at home, and all those American School of Excavation idiots." Basil had rescued her from a tea party. He had not only rescued her with the utmost tact. He had rescued poor Mrs. Defreddie as well. He had actually taken her to the party in Midget's place and had come back to the hotel with her and expounded on the party until it really seemed there might be some grain of truth in his convincing statements. "Lord, they're alive. You ought to see the tribe up at the British consulate."

Sister of Charmides. Basil had read her the Wilde poem[42] under the shadow of the extraordinarily bad statue of Verlaine in the Luxumbourg gardens. Charmides, it seems, was a youth in Greece, who fell in love with a statue.

She knew that she did not feel as he wanted her to feel, with warmth and depth and warm intensity. She knew that if she felt at all it was not with warm but with cold intensity. She did not feel for Basil with that intensity. She was forever conscious of the fact. But the comradeship was perfect. At one time she had believed that he would accept from her that comradeship and from the world what else it had to give him, but he had changed so since his years in France.

She did not mind being called sister of Charmides. She was immensely proud and flattered. But she wished that Basil had not found it out.

Yet why should it hurt? Basil's friendship was like the warmth of the setting sun thrown over the ruins of an ancient city. The sunlight of morning or noon is too dazzling against white stone. The night, too dreary, the moonlight is too ghostly. Midget had enough of the night and the pallor of the moonlight in herself. The heat of mature passion would have shriveled her. This light, as of scattered rose or of palest cyclamen, was perfect for her city. Yet primarily it was her city she loved. This light, decorative and revealing, was but second in her passion, or but as adjunct to her passion for her city. The sympathy of Basil was like a tinted robe flung over a marble image or a curtain drawn between the world and a rare treasure room.

The world had seen for centuries the Venus brought from

Milo. Yet who had seen it? Midget dared to think she saw it, white, thin, crescent shaped as in a vision, as in the first vision of the artist before his hands had bungled it in stone.

She stood before the statue in the little anteroom at the end of the long corridor of the undergallery of the Louvre, seeing the white woman with other eyes than those of the fugitive, hurried tourists, ever circling like a black whirlpool, caught in a river by a great blossoming elderbush that bends from the shelving edge of a small, threatened sandbank. So she stood, the lady, unconscious of the muddy stream about her, seeming too heavy for her pedestal, seeming to bend forward as if about to fall, great blossoming tree, into the stagnant yet ever-moving current. So they edged and moved about her, examining with far more interest the fragment of lost arm and the bit of drapery and the hand broken with its broken apple in the glass case beneath than the tall statue rearing like a white tree above them.

Here in this flow of visitors, Midget hardly dared let go realities. She dared not follow the curve of the white belly and short space before the breasts brought the curve to a sudden shadow. She hated the tribe about the pedestal. Basil hated them too, yet he had poise and wit and laughed at them. And too in some strange unexpected way he sympathized. "You'd never find little English country-school mistresses scrape and save to see these things," he said. "How pathetic your country is, and in its nasal, tight and stinted way, what love of beauty."

Basil was there to explain, to speak, to sympathize with all but the whitest passion.

But we are defrauded of the best. We have our lovers, but we do not have them in the proper setting. We are all exiles, we and they. The more joy to us, true, the greater share of glory when we meet unexpectedly in some blind alley, a little sordid, yes, by all means, a little sordid, with a street violin from not too near breathing out its *con amore* of some tawdry little opera. How they fill my heart, the tawdry, too familiar notes, how I would fill my lungs deep with them and spill them out, just breathing, from an angel's throat, how the ragged children would come trooping, rats from rats' burrows, and how from Rome and Naples white and bronze feet would step from white and bronze pedestals and steps of thrones, and we would all shout at the incongruity of us all, you and I and my lover and the ragged children and white Aphrodite and bronze Hermes and a Pan or two to divert the children and take them, more or less, off our hands and more or less out of the way.

Rome and Naples, Rome and Naples, that beats down the battered fortress of my brain.

We measure, or should measure, our capacity for life, (the depth in us for living) not by our power of attracting but by our power or possibilities of being attracted. The two, though, no doubt, like positive and negative electricities, are interdependent on one another.

This law works out with people as far as we are in a position to observe it. But as we are really ignorant of the forces, the quality of the electric forces in ourselves and in others, we are always making mistakes and blunders of our personal affairs, are coming to grief in all our personal relationships.

A work of art is the materialization of the electric force of the artist, electric force plus the directing impetus of the intellect.

The material of the sculptor is the most definite of all. His electric impulse is materialized in definite form. The dynamic strength of his original impulse should therefore reach us less encumbered (as in the other arts) with our own impulses. In music, in painting, in poetry our own emotions are apt to intrude, to cloud over the original impulse (or as commonly called, inspiration) of the artist.

We should be able, more easily, to fall in love with a statue than with any other work of art.

Rome and Naples, Rome and Naples, that beats down the battered fortress of my brain.

Not because of Rome and Naples themselves, so much, as for

all that they contain of the remote yet imminently present past. The past, too, made less formidable than the past of an Argos or Mycene or Delphi.[43] The past approachable. The past near enough; with its imperfections, human enough. We can grapple with a buried Herculaneum. We are powerless before Delphi or Olympia.[44]

To return to the Louvre. There is a god in the long Caryatid room who is very unworthy indeed. At least, as I remember him, he is plastered together from two gods. Yet he makes a very charming, very perfect friendly whole. His body, mutilated, stands firm on one shod foot while the other is placed graciously on a block of marble toward which he reaches long, slightly, I should imagine, judged by the perfect Polycleitian standard,[45] too long arms to fasten the sandal strap. This is a very charming god. I think he is called Jason fastening a sandal. His hand seems to have turned for the precise reason of observing you seated on the marble bench to the left as you enter from the long de Milo corridor.

Midget often sat on this bench. She sat there for several reasons. One, the room was not a starred Baedeker[46] room. There was nothing of supreme interest there. True, the two porphyry basins attracted the stream of muddy visitants. Baedeker has noted that a word whispered in one can be heard by anyone leaning, ear downwards, over the other.

But the stream of visitants ignored the Jason, which left Midget free for him.

On a hot summer day, the big room is very white and cool. There is a tall, white discus hurler opposite the Jason. They are both very friendly, very impersonal, very young, very sensitive, very sensible.

The Jason turned his head, I forgot to state, because his head belonged to someone else. He should really have been observing, according to all classic tradition, the sandal strap he was so graciously, with such pseudo-Attic intensity, trying to knot.

How should she praise them, these two young men, Midget used to think as she sat there. There is, it seems, a song of praise for every living statue, so for every living person in the world. The beauty of this is that every statue, as every person, draws out of us different song. Therefore our songs, had we (or have we) the gift of singing, are never at a loss for some worthy object. The trouble is not with the objects, the trouble is with ourselves.

Midget's field of attraction, her power of being attracted was somewhat limited at that time. But what she saw, she saw— having fiercely limited herself—in spite of herself.

She wanted to praise these young men. Her way of singing was curious. She sat and looked until the present was swept away like the scum on a muddy river and she was looking into the past or into the future (whichever you may prefer to call it). At least she was looking through the past and the future, as through a glass, not darkly, but with intensely luminous vision.

There was no word of praise for these young men, one quite a charming boyish youth, the other an unworthy, friendly demi-god. There were no notes to be drawn across a violin. There were no sketches to be made by exquisite amateurs. There are no imitations to be dreamed of in lesser weight of clay.

There is nothing to be done or said. But there is a great deal to be thought.

Do I become somewhat mystical in contemplation of this Midget contemplating Jason and Jason's friend, hurling his disc? That may be. But I belong to a curious race. I lived before the black cloud fell. I am living still. And while the cloud was on us, I looked and wondered and looked and did nothing to help one way or the other.

So I look at Midget now and she seems vivid to me now, more vivid than when she sat there. And the Jason and the discus hurler seem vivid, no more and no less vivid than when Midget kept them company in the White gallery, emptied of visitors with the light falling through the high palace windows, as light falls through dripping branches of fall-leafed spring trees on the early tufts of lily of the valley.

White lily of the valley. That is what I should, were I Midget with her magic gift of seeing through the present into the past or the future, whichever she may call it, place at the feet of these two heroes, make spring beneath the sandals of the one and beside the firm bare instep of the other.

I will not attempt to visualize the two as Midget saw them. But were a peculiar gift of vision granted me, a gift having nothing to do with the pen or violin or chisel, I would say: something about the firm contour of the bent torso of the Jason, something about the firm hand and the straight arm of the discus hurler, reminded me of the fresh, not-quite-opened spikes of the lily of the valley; something in the alertness of the discus hurler brought to my nostrils the scent of young birch trees but in half leaf; something about the Jason caught me like spring rain, cold, intoxicant. Something about the thought of the two of them in that half-lighted gallery brought to my soul the uttermost calm of utmost friendship, the delight of a vision of perfect understanding, without the deep fear of that friendship broken or ever being broken, the deep fear and the deep delight that comes only with infatuation.

But there is a song for every statue, and if we would follow the sister of Charmides, perhaps we must go to Rome. There is no white friendship in this statue. Midget had looked at its companion at the Louvre when there with Julia and Josepha. The small, perfect body,[47] the face turned to the wall, the curve of the small yet mature and rounded back, she had seen them first with Josepha, had been interested but not moved by this figure the poet sings of, poignantly yet with a sort of forced and artificial sweetness:

> Love stands upon thy left hand and thy right,
> Yet by no sunset and by no moonrise
> Shall make thee man and ease a woman's sighs,
> Or make thee woman for a man's delight.[48]

So it had seemed, lying there in the gallery of the palace of the Louvre, forced and artificial, a wax rose, cut from wax without fragrance, without reality or meaning. No "double rose of love's"[49] no rose at all, a blossom made of wax, not modeled even with living fingers, but poured into a set mold. At least so the statue seemed to Midget.

But here in Rome, turning one day to find a place to rest in the shadow of the wall of one of the corridors of the Diocletian gallery, she saw the little figure, yet not the same. She was startled by its beauty. It lay not on a pedestal of cold stone, but on a soft black velvet cushion, made, one could see, measured, and planned to suit this little body. It lay comfortably asleep. Midget stood looking, almost afraid to move closer. Yes, this was the same Hermaphroditus, but no little monster, no plaything of a later emperor. This was a gentle breathing image, modeled in strange, soft, honey-colored stone. The small head lay on the perfect childlike arm. It was a child, here in Rome, no monster. This was no "double rose of love's"; it was no rose at all. This was a spray of honey flower caught in the shadow of a dark wall.

A dark wall. When it was all over, the five years, and the two years it took us all to find ourselves again, to find our selves and to fasten our old selves and our new selves together, like the Jason with separate head and body, yet who makes a perfect whole, there in the Louvre, we the rebellious, the lovers of the discarded, ancient beauty, found that the war had indeed been a dark wall. A dark wall, yet for us of the old régime a background for the living, for the white future. Though we did not help to make that wall we were, after all is said and done, thankful for this sudden poignant unmistakable dividing line between the past and the future, glad that we were part of Europe and a part of the tidal wave, if only of the infinitesimal froth and fume of its crest or of its nothingness. Beneath us, the black wave might still swirl and swish with its hissings of renewed intolerance and hatred, yet on the whole the wave was drawn back into the sea, away from the lovely fields and houses and small farmsteads. The apple orchard and the little farm and the little ancient vineyard stood the same as in the days after the Persians wrecked the citadel.

There is a new citadel. Our children will see to that. But, we, the lovers of the ancient beauty, are happier than they. We endured. They will achieve. But we will be far happier than they. We are a tenuous thread swung through the reaches of the trackless forest. Fame will come to them, our children, for us the Gray Eyed grants a greater gift. She is amused with us. We are amused with her. We are the respite and the breathing space. We will be amused with our children. How they will patronize us. The Gray Eyed told me this: they will be famous, you will be happy.

SEVEN

Retrospect

So it was over, not only the peril, the suffering, the agonizing we called the war, but the years of (to some of us) even more painful period of convalescence. I mark, from my personal experience, this period of recovery as two years. We have all different invalid charts for this time of recovery. Some of us jumped up to a hectic fever heat of what seemed happiness at the first hint of the world's return to normal. Some of us went limp, when the pressure of waiting and anxiety was removed. Some of us were snuffed quietly out, many of us, in the wave of fever that caught us from the battlefields.

To us who have survived, the world stretches out, a new world, fresh, quaint, astonishingly naive. Or is it ourselves who have grown astonishingly naive, overjoyed with the taste of clean bread, with the choice of little round iced cakes or large round ones of different-colored icings. We have the pleasure, too, of crumbling perfectly fresh biscuits on the window ledge for the pigeons, and the puppies themselves are not more pleased with their square lumps of sugar than are we.

Perhaps there are many who feel as I, but I wonder how many. I am in such a peculiarly happy position. I loved Europe with such intensity and with such baffling countercurrents of pain during all the years of waiting. I trust you do not consider me "pro-German" since I make my little heroine of such a curious blend. I cannot say that I am. But I was singularly unhappy through the war. I have never, I regret, yet visited the great fatherland. But my clearest memories are of an old nurse who read me Brothers Grimm backwards and forwards and over and over and over until the book, as if touched by a magician's wand, one day fell suddenly to pieces; and the old dame said it was a sign that I had had enough of fairy stories and was grown up.

Yes, I was grown up. But still I was singularly ill informed. I labored under the delusion, for many, many years, that Hans Andersen was a German. When finally it was pointed out that Denmark was not Germany, I was still indifferent. Europe was Europe in those days. America was America. Europe has remained Europe to me to this day, though with subtle and more and more bewildering differences, not only between the different states of Europe but between the different layers of the different social strata of those different countries and their different provinces or possessions. No one but an American (I boast it) can realize the beauty and the joy of all this interflow and interchange and curious little walls of prejudice and curious little bulwarks of protection between each little class of each distinctive little walk of life.

When the pressure of active hostility was removed, many of these little social bulwarks were altogether broken down. On the other hand, certain prejudices and protective customs were curiously strengthened; almost Victorian prejudices and conventions sprang to life among the apparently advanced of the prewar period. In France, among the few acquaintances I have there, I specially note this tendency to slide back into an old layer of thought. This is no doubt perfectly natural in a country whose people were either actually swept away through death or, worse, social disaster, or who remained with one foot in the realms of civilization only by means of a severe and hostile attitude to any influence, however, under ordinary circumstances, good, that might in the least encroach upon the little stretch of sand, so to speak, left still *après le déluge,* a foothold, possibly even yet a footstep upward toward the base of the solid mountains.

Yet I judge all this superficially. I drift with the stream, since I believe the stream now to be drifting toward some ultimate land, some perfectly unintellectual land made up of the early visions of all the early poets we read when we were sixteen,[50] whom we outgrew when we were twenty and whom we find again in our peaceful thirties.

Let Midget's children, let Josepha's children look to the future, I say. Which reminds me, I am telling a story of Midget and Josepha and Basil and Raymond (who else was there?), a mysterious little Brindel yet to come and one or two others of Brindel's confrères.

How did she get through the days of the war, this Midget, you may ask, if she took no part, if she did nothing at all to help, one way or the other? It is all very well to talk, during a war. People can talk. Who dare ask us in our ordinary years what we do with ourselves, how we pass the time?

There was impertinence in the air. Midget was often asked, but what are you *doing?*

What, when it comes to that, does anyone do ever?

Midget did very little. A Zola or a de Goncourt would not have found her altogether a heroine, however, for a realistic novel. Midget thought much.

Sometimes her thought in order to escape the battle of realities went, as I have tried to show you, far too far. In order to escape judging one way or the other, Midget went perilously far out of the track of realities. But I never pretended greatness for Midget. I said that she was the froth or the nothingness of the crest of the black wave.

Yet she was no psychic. She never saw or in any way apprehended the presence of the dead, the many who had gone. If she had died, herself, in the sweep of the fever of that last year, I doubt if she would have joined the army of the dead. Whom should she have joined? I sometimes wonder. Or do we sleep after all, to wake after thousands of years?

Is there not a story current in the popular guidebooks of a little Roman, discovered during the Renaissance, lying in her patrician robes, bound with fillet of gold, with bracelets about her forearms, with small body calm and sweet with spices after all the thousand years? Is there not a story that the rabble of Rome passed before the little body, believing the girl had died but yesterday, and suddenly, as a breath of wind blew too roughly through the open doorway, the garments shriveled against the naked framework of small bones and a small skull looked out, the crown yet fastened with the yellow gold of the wrought fillet? Is there not some such tale?

Among the dead, that girl seemed near to Midget. Among the dead, Heliodora, the girl Meleager of Alexandria loved,[51] seemed living. The dead? These were not the dead, this crowd of heroes and this crowd of her own fellow beings. The rabble was not *the* dead. Or if to die was still to be among the rabble, far better live. Why not live, said Midget to herself, it is so commonplace to die.

She seems, to you, a morbid child. I have said that she was the froth or the nothingness of the crest of the deceiving breakers.

Why not live, said Midget.

The child itself, I have said, I would make of dark cypress wood, but Midget said she would make the child otherwise. As Midget always knew more of the child's heart than I, and the child was no longer anyway (at least by the Midget standards) a child, I must leave the whole to her.

She agrees with me about the pear trees. But I do not recognize the small temple she says is crowded in among them on the border of the forest. I did not know there was a forest, as a matter of fact. My Midget grew up in a garden, where the wysteria smothered down the fruit trees.

Why not live, said Midget.

She had rescued her friend[52] from the forest, at least so she said. Her friend was duly grateful. The friend was an extremely pretty creature, with eyes too intense for this generation, with bare feet too perfect, with slight arms too delicate, for all their wiry play of little nervous tendons.

"Why do you like gladiolus better than iris?" said Midget to her friend.

The friend said, "Oh, that's simple enough. I like the stalks against the wall where the sun strikes. I like the hot earth around their roots against my feet. The earth is cold where the iris grows and usually there is water prickling up."

"Prickling up," said Midget. "But water doesn't prickle."

"Water does prickle," said the friend. "Don't you know that fountain in the market square where the stones broke just because—"

"I have told you not to speak of fountains in market squares," said Midget.

"You cannot have a market square without a fountain," said the friend. "How could you bank up the wild azalea we transplanted—"

"When did we transplant?" said Midget.

"If you would sometimes remember something," grumbled Midget's friend in a petulant little voice, "I would like you much better."

"But you do, you do like me better," agonized Midget.

Her friend said, "You are not as pretty as the other girls. You do not remember. You seem stupid about the games and you cannot tie a sandal."

Said Midget, "Who would remember you, if it were not for

me? Remember yourself the beauty of your playmates, what good does that do you? Sleep in the forest or get lost in a half dream—what good does that do you? You are dead."

Midget waited for her friend to drop shuddering in an agony of weeping on the soft grass. The sun was throwing soft, just-before-setting lights across the level lawn. Midget's friend had a confusing way of calling the grass yellow. But Midget saw now that perhaps her friend was right.

The wind caught the branches of the white rose tree. The branches swung and drooped like the plumes of the wild willow. They swayed and drifted across Midget's shoulder.

The white petals drifted across Midget's rough, straight-cut peasant smock. She knew she was not charming and frail and lovely like her friend, but she was sharper, she was stronger, she was more cruel. She waited for her friend to fall sobbing on the yellow tufts of the young grass.

Her friend did not fall, nor did she sob. She bared her pretty, perfect little teeth. She straightened herself till she stood as tall as Midget. Her face was white enough. "You are a devil," she said, "my people often warned me of you. I know all about you and I am not afraid. Obviously you will fade away if I choose to waste my priestcraft on you. You are a devil, and moreover it is you who are dead."

When Midget took off her skirt, she did not look, with her long bare legs and her rough smock reaching halfway to her knees, so very unlike her lovely friend. In essentials, that is. Midget looked a little in the rough, no white rose tree, a small larch perhaps, no deciduous droop about her, a young pine perhaps.

Midget, interested always in her person, was not altogether pleased with her legs. She had always been very vain, in what we might call real life, about them and her level shoulders and her throat and especially her chin. Now as she considered her friend, kneeling in the other end of the canoe, she felt singularly modest, and for Midget, singularly unsatisfied with her (until this moment) to herself, singularly fascinating physical appearance.

The trouble was, thought Midget, there was no one, really, much to compare oneself to. At least no one to observe continually in the open or wherever one wants, or however one wants. There was Josepha (why isn't she here?), of course. But I never saw her out of doors, and anyhow Julia seemed to think us queer for wanting to see each other walking around the room in Bloomsbury, and when we tried to get some photographs in that old boat at Etaples, Julia shouted there was a man (and a *French* man) coming and we must get dressed at once. It was all interrupted. One was just learning the feel of that young sage and that brambly, dwarf heather on the souls of one's feet, and Julia kept persisting that even our shoes must go on and we must hurry as the man was looking. Never found out anything that mattered.

"We bathed in clothes," said Midget to her friend, "a skirt and a top piece."

Midget's friend was by this time so bored by various details Midget had given her of the conditions of what we might call real life that she was not even revolted by this last disgusting item.

"If I die," she remarked philosophically, "I may go to Hell but it will be my own people's Hell, no whorepen of the rabble."

The word she really used was not whorepen but that is as translatable as I can find.

"I think you are mistaken," said Midget, "somewhat prejudiced in your ideas."

The canoe was drawn up, half out of the little salt-marsh backwater of a stream they had paddled into from the bay. They were resting on a narrow stretch of terra firma, a shelf cutting sheer from the marsh. The thick grass stood firm and tall. On the very edge, nearest their own particular little bank, the spikes were brown a little, and coarse. They grew greener toward the marsh edge. There they stood, the first foot or so, with their graduated tideline, marked on each individual blade, a rim of salt. The blades stood in shallow water, then half covered. Then the marsh ceased by an imperceptible graduation and became the stream itself. However, at the moment, the tide being exactly at the ebb, there was scarcely a ripple of the sea grass beneath the surface. The sea grass and the marsh grass seemed to blend. Unless you straightened yourself and became alert and squinted carefully, you could scarcely have stated offhand where the marsh ended and the sea began. But a long heron saved Midget and her friend the trouble of consciously exerting themselves. A flap from the very particular twist of the little creek upon which their eyes had been fastened in a half-dream, and they were alert and fully conscious with no effort, as I have said, on their own part, no exertion of their minds or their bodies.

They made no remark on the heron and his flight. Midget repeated, "I think you are mistaken."

It had never been Midget's practice to stand up for her own country when she heard it abused in common conversation. She had never entered into discussion of any kind, on the comparative merits of France, Austria, Germany, England, and the outlying etceteras of the Balkans and Russia and the rest of them. She was not, in the commonly accepted use of the term, what you would call a patriotic girl. But she found suddenly in her dealings with her friend a new loyalty. She found she was loyal. She had always felt that she had missed a great deal during the war by being so totally devoid of that quality that seemed to make everyone more or less happy, or important in a tragic way, or at least at one with their fellow beings and their environment. Midget found that she was loyal. She even transposed the term in her transport of discovery. She said to herself, "Now I know what it feels like. I am patriotic."

She was not patriotic as you or I should use or understand the term. But she had a sense of loyalty to the world of what we call, real life, at large. When her friend began abusing the real world, Midget became warm about the jaw bone. She was uncommonly interested in this new sensation. She knew now what so many people had felt, all over the world. This she had not felt before. She was feeling patriotic. The world is a country, she thought, and I do not wish to see the world perish. I do not wish to see the world knocked out by another world. Yes, I am patriotic. This is the way my landlady in Bloomsbury used to feel about England and Germany.

"And about modernity," she thought. "That is a horrid word Althea used." (I do not know that the child's name was Althea but Midget called her that.)

"You are limited in your outlook," said Midget.

The tide was thrusting against the grass blades. There was a little hiss, and each new wavelet seemed to gain impetus from some unknown power or some unapparent stream or undercurrent of force beneath the water. The tide had turned, was well toward the way to drowning out the little tide marks on the grass. The upper grass was half under water.

The warm bank beneath their bodies, though well heated through by the all-day sunlight, seemed suddenly not so warm. The sun was still high in heaven and there was no cloud observable, but Midget gave a little shudder. She sat up. She observed that her elbow was raw and she saw that she had been leaning heavily on a root but insufficiently padded by the soft mold and half-broken fragments of last year's sun-baked leaves.

Althea was standing. She had carefully tucked her skirt into the belt that fastened just below the armpits. Her legs were as bare, though not so brown as Midget's. She unfastened the belt and let the whole garment fall loose, the better to shake out the bits of twig and leaf and pine needles that were scratching her thigh and the half of her back where she had been resting her shoulder. The garment hung heavy in ample, gracious folds. So she stood beneath the one pine outstanding from the scrub pine and small cornel and deciduous oak and young sassafras that edged the forest.

Midget, the whole time they had been resting there, had been ruminating. She was thinking of the beauty of the world. She was remembering. The black cloud that had been the war had lifted. The evil it had brought her, the despair, the pain were gone. She remembered of all the countries of the world, the one she seemed at the moment to love the best. "London— gives one, as no city in the world gives one, a background."

This world where she had wandered, where she met and rescued her lovely friend, had more to give, was far more beautiful than any stray corner of England, even excepting Cornwall. This world of her dreams, the place where she found herself in her own most ardent moments, was America, not the country she had left so long since with Josepha, but that country enriched, hardened, deepened, civilized, with all the vigor of its wildernesses plus some ancient quality of finesse, some patrician sense of uttermost discrimination. America was, as it now was, a perfect haven, undeniably a refuge for the mediocre. The golden, comfortable commonplace drew to it and comforted those not too uncomfortable. But she had been too uncomfortable, she and Josepha and such as she and Josepha. What of Althea, the white future, yet unborn? Orient pearls, were they to be washed forever and forever toward the feet of the old world?

She had prepared her little speech for white Althea. "Ah, the garden, if you could but see it after the rain!"

"He was one of those for whom the visible world exists,"—a much-quoted quotation. Midget was not, or had not been during the period of her stormy adolescence, one of those for whom the visible world exists. The visible world in childhood had existed for her, in all its depth and breadth, in all its tropic summer heat and in its winter of Norwegian snow and ice storm that covered the trees; the ice and snow of the far north with lights playing purple in snowdrifts and iridescent blues and dark blues across each tiny ice-covered twig and embryonic shape of coming bud and tassel of the sweeping, almost breaking, but so wonderfully just enduring, resilient forest birches.

Summer and winter exist in the visible world for the American of the middle eastern Atlantic seaboard states. And spring is a hectic feverish tyrant. Denied expression during all the paralyzing winter, it trails suddenly with all its panoply, with all its attendant beauties. Too suddenly, too beautifully for any but a child's heart to endure. Midget came, in her early twenties, to hate the spring with its overly effusive glamor, its cherries sprung over night into full, deep-wadded bloom, to perish over night in a forced blight, a heat blight you might have thought, but that the young, almost mature leaves did their utmost to hide the ragged, sodden balls of withered blossoms.

But in England the spring came with tact, with insinuating charm. Did it ever go, when it comes to that? Is not England a land of almost perpetual promise, and you might add, were you one of Midget's satirical acquaintances, with almost perpetual unfulfillment of promise? True the small figs never came to fruitage. True, the peaches and apricots were (judged by her American standards) uneatable. Grapes, ripened occasionally with much coaxing and pruning and cherishing against especially sheltered walls. But what of all this? The spring came with the first lamb's tails, the small plumage of the willow, and the early town crocuses and windowbox snowdrops and first hyacinth, in February sometimes. While it was a Christmas game for the children to find a bouquet in late December, a rose or so, some spray of sturdy northern jasmine, even a stalk of next spring's premature narcissus.

Spring came in England with a certain gracious footfall. It did not dance, for all the poets sing of proud-pied April and the daffodils. It stepped, like a gracious lady, like Aphrodite civilized, gracious, not too young (well, in the late twenties), tall, simply robed, robed in the utmost taste. No vulgar display. No vying to outdo her neighbors.

Ah, spring, said Midget, I can sit on a bench for three months and watch you come, and then you have only just arrived. For another three months, I can think and ruminate and wonder at it all and at you yourself. How is it you put up with me, an outcast, a barbarian lady?

The lady said nothing to Midget. But it was almost as if the great tufts of licac, pale and white and deep purple, royal, magnificent small trees, took a deeper tinge, took a sharper outline. So the lady might have stood, alert, her face gone white. For "I love you," said Midget.

Ah, the garden if you could but see it, Althea. It is as if the whole thing were rounded, just big enough to grapple with. There is no use trying to grapple with things in this country. "And may the inner and the outer be at peace." There is no use praying that prayer in America. It is all too big, too unformed, too impersonal. Here in the garden, you can grapple with the whole, make it conform to oneself or make oneself conform to it.

The inner and the outer are at peace. If one were a god one might have made this garden.

It is true we are hedged off from the grass, but that makes the vision of the grass, of the shrubbery beyond and of the bordering flowers more apart from oneself and more of oneself.

We jog one another's shoulders, the whole circling crowd of us. We walk up one side of the broad path and down the other. The broad path is divided in the middle by a row of trees. There are bunches along the line; small green chairs and an occasional little armchair or a pair of little armchairs make a little hedge or borderline between the two, the going up and the going down part of the path. Yet the stream going up and the stream going down are more or less ambling on of their own volition. We cross between openings in the little barricade of chairs. We wander down with the up crowd and we wander up with the down crowd. This is so pleasant and English. In America (if such a park as Hyde Park could be imagined as existing in America) the crowd would rush and push and get in one another's way, and there would be no peaceful resting on the little green chairs. There would be jumpings up and sittings down and hailings of people in rather pronounced voices from distances. In the great fatherland, I imagine, there would be valiant guards of one sort or another, to add, it is true, reclame to the scene, but to make a more or less set tradition (because a more or less new tradition) of the goings up and the comings down and please do not pass between the benches in the little spaces which are not made for this purpose but happen more or less by accident. In France, I do not know. But I do not think this special sort of crowd would find time for such harmonious wandering in the open.

Above our heads, the great branches form a splendid canopy. An iron railing, a broad space of half the walk, the trees, the benches between the trees, the other half of the walk and another railing. This is the order of the lines. Yes, there is a row of benches, I forgot, placed with their backs against the first iron railing. Then there is the row proper. A very wide road, this. Here are the horses. My dear Althea, I wish I had the nerve to ride in the row. There are some very bad riders. This generation of girls does not ride as well as the last, I am told. The war took the horses. But now they look so friendly and charming and not in such terrifyingly good form. Most of the men look extremely smart. The men look better as a whole than the women. Most of the girls wear riding breeches now and, between ourselves, you must be very smart and slim and well knit to look your best in breeches and a short coat. But then as I say, it is all friendly and not terrifying. I used to freeze with terror before the war, when I chanced on a beautiful English-woman, walking or riding. I felt I moved in the wrong way, jerked with nerves, had no poise.

Well, the riders ride, rather fiercely and wildly, some of them. At least at the end of the row, there is usually a little fiery group that has raced (within the prescribed, rather generous time limit) the last length. They come bouncing and pawing in. Then they rein up their steeds and walk back, calmly, the up and down, in no way interfering, all making a friendly circle, we walking and they riding. They the mighty ones are set apart from us, yet we ourselves feel somehow not at all out of things, as if by leaning on the rail and watching, we were a part of the circle within the rail, the more lordly circle of men and privileged young women and the kingly steeds.

There is something in these English people that (now that the war is over) is essentially respectful toward the privacy and the personal affairs of others. Certain of my satirical London acquaintances say that this is not, *au fond*, respect but crass selfishness. Be that as it may, the result is the same. I can wear any kind of clothes I want, good ones or old ones. I can sit on one of the little green chairs for an hour alone, just ruminating, and no one speaks to me, or looks at me or seems to be saying to themselves as they pass for the fifth or sixth time on the up and down promenade, "It's too bad her admirer has deserted her." Alone or with an escort, one is equally shielded and apart.

Althea, this is a little tirade on the beauties of the visible world. The visible world exists; I have found since I have outgrown the period of war convalescence that the visible world exists as poignantly, as etherially as the invisible. There is another world, or a combining of two worlds. When we can get the visible and the invisible together that makes another world. I used to believe in the past and in what I called the future; when you get the past and the future together you get what I call, now for the sake of argument, the present, at least a poignant and ethereal present which I call the visible world.

There are hours and hours which are drab nothingness. I used to call this the "present which is dead." There is a present which is dead, there is also the living present.

EIGHT

Visible World

ALTHEA was standing. She had stood attentively for a long time, one hand resting with bent wrist just below the hip, the other, serving as a prop for the chin, outthrust a very little, balancing the droop forward of the serious forehead. The garment, fresh fastened at the waist, fell almost to the ankles. The two feet were fastened firm on the ground. Althea looked serious, not so childlike, a woman.

"I do not understand your philosophy," she said. "I do not think I should like your garden, your trees, your people, your horses. I have listened to many arguments on the origin of the world, of space and of the stars. I have not yet heard a plea, or a defense, as you seem to have made it, of the visible world. If you must argue about and defend your so-called visible world, I do not think it can be a very pleasant, satisfying, or convincing place to live in. In fact, I do not understand you at all. You seem to be talking in a cloud, about a cloud. Is your world a cloud, that you must make these curious distinctions between past, present, visible and invisible?"

Midget was wading toward the canoe. She was swaying the light prow backwards and forwards in order to loosen it from the sedge, though the tide had already lifted it almost free. The incoming wavelets caught and splashed the hem of her heavy tunic, weighting it still heavier against her bare upper legs; but Midget did not notice. Her head was thrown back. Her nostrils were taut with the inbreath of a new layer of storm wind. She drew the canoe parallel with the grasses, up tilted toward the shore. "Get in," she said.

"It is too late," said the girl.

They had spread their garments to dry in the other room. There was a smoldering brazier there. The marble about the feet of the tripod was baked warm. They spread their clothes there to dry.

The little outer room was rather sultry. The downpour of rain seemed to shut like a solid gray curtain across the low windows reaching to the floor, opening out into the veranda or porch set with white pillars. The rain seemed to be swung like a curtain between the pillars, so straight, so heavy was its fall.

They had shaken out their garments and little scraps of leaves, pine needles, bits of bramble and twig lay scattered about the floor. Midget was shaking her head violently in her effort to shake out the rain and the uncomfortable twigs yet adhering. Her body was warm and dry but her head was a damp wad of rain-soaked stringy locks. Althea had wrapped a fold of her garment about her when the storm commenced and her head appeared sleek and beautiful in its very slight disarray.

"You are very tall," she said. "The tunic you wear shows all the worst of your body. Your legs are too thin but perhaps you will outgrow that."

Midget gasped. "I am completely grown," she said.

"They let you grow wrong somewhere," said her friend.

Althea was not like a statue, not like a statue in a museum, that is. Yet, after all, statues in museums never have a chance, and Althea was showing to the very best advantage. She was standing on the whortle berry-colored blanket. (They had dragged it in from the little hall.) The red blanket showed up the white feet with the little marks of the crisscross of the sandal strap. The white body of Althea showed a deeper rose than it was really as contrasted with the marble wall at her back. The line of the frieze cut the wall two-thirds from the floor. The ceiling was very low. The line of the frieze cut just below Althea's shoulders.

The frieze was done in some dull gold design. The line of the drawing was lost in the darkness, but here and there flecks of gold glinted out as the flames of the brazier glowed now and then more intensely in the shadow.

"You are not altogether beautiful," said Althea, "but you look alive."

"I am alive," said Midget.

They had pushed through the scrub and low bushes after they had dragged the canoe ashore and wedged it between two saplings. They had pulled and tugged, exerting themselves, valiant in their youth and intense with necessity for swift but defined and solid action. They had left the canoe safe. They might themselves have crawled under the hollow of the boat husk, as it uptilted, slightly lifted on one side by the less resilient trunk of the larger little tree. But the magnetic slash of light and the deep distant roar acted on them like the roll of drums to the peacesated warrior or the Celtic pipes to the shepherd, tired of sheeptending on the hills, and they were off, swift, light of limb, with intent purpose. Their purpose, they could not have put into words. The last thing that urged them was the fear of being overtaken by the storm. They seemed, rather, though fleeing in the direction opposite to that of the swiftly rising cloud bank, to be facing an enemy, long expected. There was joy in them such as comes to the heart when certainty is upon us, after hours of tension and enervating unsatisfied expectancy.

Babies they were, girls or boys, with the wind about their bodies, with their slight shoulders set against the sometimes almost inpenetrable wall of green that met them, half-blinded with wind and slash of rain. One would push through, the other burrow after. Then there would be a clear space for some yards and they would pause a moment, take a deep breath and be lost between thick pine trunks. The feel of it. The bite and tear and sting of it. Yet what joy is there in loneliness. All the power of the wood seemed to circle between those two alert and vivid bodies, like two shafts attracting the two opposite currents of the electric forces of the forest.

It needs two or more than two to make a living prayer of the passion of swift feet, of the passion of struggling tall white young bodies, of the passion of intense young faces, uplifted to the dash of rain and the more cruel interpiercing of rare hailstones. Two or three and a living prayer. Two on three and that most passionate of passions, the innate chastity of the young, the living spirits of the untouched, sacred virgins of Artemis.

Midget was indeed alive and Althea, her companion, was alive. Their young bodies were worn out with the tussle, the valiant tussle and valiant defeat of the pursuing elements. They were proud and young and alive.

Moreover, to us, considering their several merits, wondering at them, with their feet tucked under them, savagewise, seated at either end of the low, wide couch in the larger room opening out from the little brazier-heated anteroom where they had left their rougher outer garments, moreover to us, considering them, they were beautiful.

"What is beauty," said Althea to Midget.

"Beauty," said Midget to Althea, "is proportion."

"Then all things are beautiful," said Althea.

"All things become beautiful if we, through the creative use of the intellect, transform them by a process of resetting them or reconsidering them in relation to what they have been or, more important still, to what they may become. Nothing is static. All things change."

"You and I change?"

"You and I change," said Midget, "but the creative mind in us does not alter. You and I grow old but never to ourselves unsightly, if within us, the creative intellect, remains intact, unchanged, unchanging."

"Our gods are not so different," said Althea, "though our worlds are worlds apart."

"Our worlds are not so many worlds apart. In the London garden I meet you. I stand against the inner rail of the wide walk I told you of. Behind me, the crowd flows and flows, one directing force inspiring the whole body of the people. Perhaps not a great nor inspiring force, but a friendly force, and when a crowd of people move backwards and forwards with even pace and serenity, some force emanates from them, some force not evil; some god, not a god of ours perhaps, not a god of the beauty-loving nor an individualistic god, but a deity for all that, not to be ignored in our litany to all the gods."

"This god is the plebeian god."

"He is the god of the plebeian, but the surest aristocrat recognizes and does him homage. It is only the unsure, the nouveau who fears to do justice to the people's god."

"The people do not do justice to the god of the aristocrat."

"That is no reason why the aristocrat, with his clearer intellect, his more mellow and seasoned outlook, should not do justice (with slightly cynical though with all humorous reservations) to the deity of the people."

"The people would trample our gods to death, if they could see them."

"If they could see them, they would cease to be the people. They would be, like ourselves, aristocrats."

"If they could see them. They cannot see them."

Midget corrected her. "They will not see them."

"But," added Midget, "the people moving serene in a compact group are protected and befriended by this emanating force we have called the god of the people. There is no need to fear unduly for their safety. It is such as ourselves who are in danger."

"But danger whets our will," said the girl, "and danger is the serpent curled in worship at the feet of the Athenians' goddess, and danger is the Python conquered by the Delphian[53] and danger is the lure calling the gods to earth, and it is only danger that summons the twins from heaven, Castor and Pollux,[54] on their snow-white horses."

Althea had slid gracefully but with a certain immature angularity off the low couch onto the floor. She gained an uncertain footing among the shadows. Then she stood upright. She raised her two white arms and stretched her supple body.

"Those horses," she said, "you spoke of. Are they snow white like the steeds of the brother stars?"

And memories came to Midget. Memories of the days when the London gardens were a green sponge, treacherous to catch, to strangle one, like evil growth of tangling weeds under treacherous waters. Memories came to Midget. The war. Her own youth. The long hours when her shoulders ached with bending over a school arithmetic or a dreary uninspiring volume of what was called Ancient History. Ancient History. What had they taught her of the Delphian and the goddess of the Precipice? What had they told her of the stars and the brothers on their horses? What had they told her of Althea and the fountains in the market and the wild azaleas?

Midget had said "beauty is proportion." Her brave mind and her valiant spirit grew black with memories. "Ugliness is disproportion," her soul spoke, "and the world is ugly."

She too stood upon the floor, but hers was a defiant and a steady step among the shadows. Althea was right, but Althea should not know that she was right.

"I stand against the inner rail. I am alone, but being quietly among the people I gain a certain surety from their moving numbers. My clothes are like their clothes. My thoughts are like their thoughts. But I, being one of your—if only one of the very least of your—people, have my creative intellect apart from my thoughts and their thoughts, apart from their god. They do not annoy me and the presence of their god does not interfere with me, provided I conceal from them the fact that I have a creative intellect, a thing they do not possess nor care to possess, and provided I do not use that creative intellect to thwart their purposes, or to endanger or belittle the being of their god.

"I stand against the inner rail and our worlds are not so many worlds apart. The sward beyond the rail is close and green save under the far trees, where it has been left wild and free in homage to the tall blue hyacinths that grow there. These patches of wild grass and spikes of hyacinth rise like islands in the short grass. Between the great trees there is a space of bushes and low trees. Lilac, low white thorn and pink May. Beneath the small trees there are thick little patches of full, very round pink and white daisies—English daisies we always called them as children. There are spikes of lupine, showing purple though not yet in flower.

"Where there is a garden, where there is a patch of untrod grass, there is a god, not solely a patron of the people. They have made a statue, even they whom you scorn, of the deity, the goddess with shaft and bow, standing in bronze in the center of the sward. About her feet the pigeons peck and splatter in the basin from which rises the pedestal she stands on."

"Who is this goddess?"

Midget answered, "Artemis."

Althea yawned. She asked, "And Aphrodite?"

Midget knew she was defeated. She said, "There is no Aphrodite."

I must leave them there; their worlds, I think, are not so very many worlds apart. What of my world and your world? Are we worlds and worlds apart from their world, are we worlds apart from one another? *Cras amet qui numquam amavit.* Let him love today who never has loved. Has loved? Who has ever loved? Among the dead.

"Thou wert the morning star among the living." Genoa and the smooth bay and the small boat.[55] Genoa and the sea roughened and the boat tossed and menaced in the wind. Genoa and the Italian blue gone treacherous with banked clouds. The small boat and the poet struggling with the tangled rope and the sail blown like a wet leaf against the mast, ropes loose and the white cloth flapping, caught in the opposite current of storm wind. "Thou wert the morning star among the living." So Shelley had translated it from Plato. Who had loved among the living? Among the dead, Plato had loved and had been drawn in the end to the white star that had been his lover on the earth. Shelley. Plato. Genoa. The boat capsized and the poet's body washed ashore.

Midget had stood with Basil beside the slab that marked his place among the dead. Among the living. Above their heads the tall avenue of camellias met and shut out the clear light of the blue Italian winter or spring heaven. Midget read the words inscribed on the stone beneath the poet's name. "He hath suffered a sea change into something rich and strange."[56] A sea change.

The white camellias and the pink camellias marked the clear gravelly earth of the wide path with rosettes of petal, pink and white like the pink and white candles on a child's birthday cake. The walk, the flowers, the peak of the pyramid of stone sacred to Caius Cestus showing beside the single cypress shaft beyond the wall, it was all, even at the time, remotely romantic, something not to be believed though one stood actually on the walk and crunched, beneath one's feet, the pebbly earth and gathered an armful of the fallen flowers and placed them, a circle, pink then white, pink then white, pink then white, around the inscription on the stone marking the poet's place among the dead.

Midget and Basil lived. They loved, I suppose one would say. Yet they seem infinitely remote and unbelievable beside the Midget of the long legs and the short tunic and the rain-wet stringy locks. They seem infinitely remote beside a Midget arguing for beauty with a white Althea yet unborn.

Midget and Josepha lived. They loved, I suppose one might say. But theirs was a remote and impossible sisterhood, ghostly with the ghost pigeons upon the windowsill at Liverpool, ghostly and unreal as the mammoth *Maurisitimania* waiting in the dingy harbor to separate them, ghostly as the sulphurous substance they call in London winter, fog.

Midget and Josepha loved. That is obvious. A small amber-colored being crept into Midget's life, a creature unbelievable, far less convincing than white Althea. A creature, white as a camellia, amber as a honeybee, black as a gypsy's baby. White and black, amber and camellia white, not to be believed yet easily proved as existent by cupping its firm black head in the hollow of a hand and watching it laugh, clutching with a hummingbird's claw. I have seen with my own eyes the creature. I know that it exists.

Midget and Josepha loved. I have not seen the mythical beings that make up the sum total of Josepha's present interest in humanity, the arts, the world at large, but I have heard they too exist.

Cras amet qui nunquam amavit. I have said that there is a Brindel yet to come. She is the one with the white future. She says, "I do not like Midget's arguments but Althea's." She is one with the past, trailing purple and vanity and despair and tragedy and dirth. She is one with the small people with hummingbird claws that are so hard for me to realize. She understands and explains them to me.

Let him love today who never has loved, for tomorrow, who knows where flits the creature of his loving.

(In preparation, *White Althea.*)[57]

Notes to the Text

Note: The first four chapters of *Paint It Today*, edited by Susan Stanford Friedman and Rachel Blau DePlessis, were published in *Contemporary Literature* 27 (Winter 1986): 444–74.
1. *small Hermione.* H.D. was probably thinking both of Helen's child, Hermione, in Greek mythology and of Shakespeare's queen in *The Winter's Tale*, who was forced into hiding after her husband, King Leontes, condemned her to death.
2. *Hera and Artemis.* Goddesses of Greek mythology. Hera, Zeus's queen, is the goddess of marriage and childbirth. Artemis, the goddess of the Amazons, is chaste and scorns the love of men.
3. *irreverent male youth.* Based on the American poet Ezra Pound, 1885–1972, to whom H.D. was briefly engaged in their native Pennsylvania. Later called "Raymond" in the text.
4. *She had failed in her college career.* H.D. withdrew from Bryn Mawr in her sophomore year because of failing grades.
5. *Paul of Tarsus.* Saint Paul. Acts 22.6 in Gal., "As I made my journey and drew near to Damascus, about noon a great light from heaven suddenly shown upon me."
6. *Josepha.* Based on Frances Josepha Gregg, H.D.'s friend and lover while in her twenties. H.D. and Gregg traveled to Europe with Gregg's mother in 1911.

7. *Valeria Messalina.* Third wife of Emperor Claudius; she was executed for promiscuity and bigamy.

8. *The hounds of Hecate.* Hounds guarding the gates of the Underworld, the province of Goddess Hecate in Greek mythology. Hecate was associated with dark deeds and witchcraft; the Greek poets regarded her as the "dark" aspect of Artemis.

9. *Cras amet.* From an anonymous Latin poem: *"Cras amet qui numquam amavit, quique amavit cras amet!"* (Let those love now, who never loved before: let those who always loved, now love the more.)

10. *qui numquam amavit.* See note 9.

11. *the swallow wing.* H.D. often referred to lyric poetry as a "swallow" song after one of her favorite poems by Swinburne, "Itylus," in which Philomel calls to her "sister swallow," Procne. H.D. and Gregg associated the poem with their "sister" love.

12. *I have come again away from the dead,/. . . Too much of yourself to me.* H.D.'s translation of Heine. I have been unable to find this passage in Heine's work.

13. *quique amavit.* See note 9.

14. "Thou wert the morning star among the living/ . . . New splendor to the dead." British poet Percy Bysshe Shelley's translation of Plato which forms the epithet for Shelley's elegy to Keats, *Adonais.*

15. *Andros, or Arcadia or Helenis.* Probably H.D.'s invention of conceivable names for ancient Greek ships, which were often named after their native regions.

16. *my companion.* Based on British novelist, poet, essayist, and translator Richard Aldington (later called "Basil" in the text). Aldington and H.D. were married in 1913, separated in 1919, and divorced in 1938. He, H.D., and Ezra Pound were all part of the "Imagist" artistic movement that peaked just before World War I.

17. *"Arma virumque . . . cano."* First line of Virgil's Greek epic *The Aenead,* "I sing of arms and the man."

18. *Theocritus.* Early Greek poet that Midget is presently translating. H.D. claimed that her first volume, *Sea Garden,* was inspired by his poetry.

19. *Amrayllis in the shade.* Line 69 of John Milton's *Lycidas:* "To sport with Amaryllis in the shade."

20. *Liddell and Scott.* Standard Greek-English lexicon.

21. *Faustine.* A nickname for Josepha that derives from Swinburne's poem "Faustine" in *Poems and Ballads*, about a debauched Roman-empress femme fatale.

22. *Ah, tausend Rosen, tausend, tausend Rosen.* Line from Richard Aldington's poem, "Reflections": "A thousand roses, a thousand, thousand roses."

23. *Oh roses of Paestum.* From Richard Aldington's poem, "Reflections." H.D. also quotes the line throughout her short story, "Murex," in *Palimpsest* (Carbondale: Southern Illinois University Press, 1917).

24. *wall, moonlight, peasblossom.* Scattered references from Shakespeare's *A Midsummer-Night's Dream*. H.D. uses the figure of the wall to express the devastation wreaked by war on her formerly unfettered girlhood "self."

25. *He gives University Extension lectures.* Frances Gregg wrote to H.D. in 1912 that she was going to marry lecturer Louis Wilkinson. She asked H.D. to accompany them to Brussels, but Pound stopped her at the train station from going.

26. *"She is in love with that Irish dramatist."* Gregg's marriage was merely an arrangement so that she could be near the man she really loved, novelist Llewelyn Powys.

27. *Leukothea.* A sea goddess in Greek mythology. Aldington often referred to H.D. similarly as the Greek goddess "Astrea."

28. *Orestes.* Son of Clytemnestra and Agamemnon in Greek mythology. Orestes was ordered by Apollo to avenge his father's death by killing his mother, who had slain the king upon his return from the Trojan War. Midget uses Orestes as a figure for her "Oedipal" conflict with her mother.

29. *Yet she was not Electra, the sister, who waited.* Electra waited patiently for her brother Orestes to return from hiding and plotted with him to slay their mother. Overcome by filial guilt, Midget cannot identify herself with the heroism of either Electra or Orestes.

30. *There was a war.* World War I.

31. *lost her companion.* H.D. and Aldington were separated in 1919 after he became involved with Dorothy Yorke.

32. *Cerebrus might have yapped at Psyche sent on her mission into Hell.* Psyche, daughter of a king in Greek mythology, was ordered

by a cruel goddess to perform a number of tasks, which included a visit to the Underworld. There, Cerebrus, the dog guarding the gates of Hades, might have "yapped" at her.

33. *Italia. Thou hast the fatal gift of beauty.* George Gordon Byron, chap. 2, stanza 42, *Childe Harold's Pilgrimage:* "Italia! Oh Italia! thou who hast/ the fatal gift of beauty."

34. *the pot of basil.* A ridiculing play on Basil's name which equates him with the beheaded lover in Keats's poetic rendering of a story from Boccaccio's *Decameron*, "Isabella: or the Pot of Basil." Isabella's greedy brothers kill and bury her beloved Lorenzo; but she unearths his head and lovingly plants it in a pot of basil, which she affectionately deems her "Basil-Pot" (LXI, 1.96).

35. *Catullus.* Gaius Valerius Catullus, a Roman poet who imitated Sappho and is known chiefly for his poems to his mistress, Lesbia. Although Midget appears to be describing a fictive male lover, the reference suggests female homoeroticism.

36. *Thy hyacinth hair . . . Ah, Psyche, from the regions which.* From Edgar Allen Poe's "To Helen" (lines 7 and 14), a favorite of H.D.'s.

37. *hyacinths.* For H.D., as well as a tradition of Romantic/Victorian poets, references to hyacinths or to Hyacinth often encode homoeroticism. In Greek mythology the beautiful boy Hyacinth was slain by Apollo accidentally during a discus-throwing contest. Apollo mourned his beloved Hyacinth's death by creating a flower out of the boy's blood. References to Hyacinth and hyacinths appear frequently in H.D.'s poetry and prose.

38. *Helen thy beauty.* From the first line of Poe's "To Helen."

39. Do you remember how you made me say "Swallow" to you . . . "thy way is long to the sun and the south" . . . "the wild birds take flight and follow and find the sun?" From Swinburne's "Itylus," which Midget mistakenly calls "Swallow." Swinburne's poem, which emphasizes the sisters' love for one another in the myth of Procne and Philomel, was a favorite of H.D.'s. See note 11.

40. *cede virgo Delia.* The maid of Delos; Artemis.

41. *sister of Charmides.* In a story by the Roman poet Lucian, Charmides falls in love with a statue of Aphrodite. H.D. derives the title from Oscar Wilde's poem about the legend, "Charmides," in which "statue-love" (my phrase) encodes transgressive (homoerotic) desire. H.D.'s references to Midget as a "sister of Charmides" refers

both to her homoerotic desires and to her coalescence of eroticism with "cold" aesthetic passion.

42. *the Wilde poem.* See note 41.

43. *Argos or Mycene or Delphi.* Cities in ancient Greece.

44. *Herculaneum . . . Delphi or Olympia.* Respectively, the city of Herculaneum in ancient Greece, which was buried by Mount Vesuvius in 79 A.D., the city of the Delphic oracle, and the Olympic dwelling of the gods.

45. *Polycleitian standard.* Standard set by Polycleitus, early Greek sculptor and architect.

46. *Baedeker.* Karl Baedeker was the author of a series of guidebooks to Europe.

47. *the small, perfect body.* The statue of the *Hermaphrodite* in the Diocletian gallery. H.D. visited the statue frequently when in Rome and kept a reproduction of it in her home.

48. *Love stands . . . for a man's delight.* From Swinburne's poem, "Hermaphroditus," which depicts the hermaphrodite as a tragic figure, neither male nor female.

49. *double rose of love's.* From Swinburne's poem "Fragoletta," portraying male androgyny as a "doubling" rather than a negation of sexualit(ies).

50. *the early poets . . . sixteen.* Probably the pre-Raphaelite poets whose poetry Ezra Pound introduced to the young H.D. and H.D. read with Frances Gregg—D. G. Rossetti, A. C. Swinburne, and William Morris in particular.

51. *Heliodora, the girl Meleager . . . loved.* Heliodora is the idealized woman in the work of the Greek lyric poet, Meleager. Although a poet in her own right, Heliodora is known exclusively as the beloved in Meleager's poetry. H.D. entitled her 1924 volume of poetry, *Heliodora.*

52. *her friend.* Based on H.D.'s longtime companion Bryher (Winifred Ellerman) (later called "Althea" in the text), whom H.D. met in 1918. The daughter of a British shipping magnate, Bryher wrote a number of historical novels and financially helped several writers and artists, including H.D. She adopted H.D.'s daughter, Perdita, and the three of them lived together on and off until 1946.

53. *the Python conquered by the Delphian.* The Greek god Apollo slew the python, a monster who once lived in the caves of Parnassus.

54. *Castor and Pollux*. Twin gods in Greek mythology who rode snow-white horses and who were the protectors of sailors and warriors in battle. They are associated with the twin stars, Gemini.

55. *Genoa and the small boat*. The following passage imaginatively re-creates Shelley's death by drowning while sailing his boat on the coast of Genoa.

56. *a sea change into something rich and strange*. From Shakespeare's *The Tempest* (I, ii). Ariel tells Prince Ferdinand (falsely) that his father is dead.

57. *White Althea*. Here the manuscript breaks off. H.D. indicated that she planned to write a succeeding section, "White Althea," which would include the child, Brindel, and, perhaps, affect the final union of the "visible" and "invisible" worlds to which Midget aspires.